Saint Padre Pio

In the Footsteps of Saint Francis

Michael J. Ruszala

D1129068

About the Author

Michael J. Ruszala holds an M.A. in Theology and Christian Ministry and a B.A. in Philosophy and Theology *summa cum laude* from Franciscan University of Steubenville. Certified as a parish catechetical leader by the Diocese of Buffalo, he is Director of Lifelong Faith Formation at St. Pius X Catholic Church in Getzville, NY. Michael has served as an adjunct lecturer in religious studies at Niagara University in Lewiston, NY, and as a member of several catechetical committees for the Diocese of Buffalo. An active member of the Society of Catholic Social Scientists and author of several religious books, he has been published in religious journals including the *Social Justice Review,* the *Catholic Social Science Review,* and *Lay Witness* online edition. With interests in music, art, tennis, and kayaking, Michael also enjoys directing the children's choir at his parish.

"Jesus is with you even when you don't feel His presence. He is never so close to you as He is during your spiritual battles. He is always there, close to you, encouraging you to fight your battle courageously. He is there to ward off the enemy's blows so that you may not be hurt."

– St. Pio of Pietrecina, August 15, 1914

Foreword

In an age that smirks at the mention of miracles, sin, angels, and demons, St. Pio of Pietrecina has emerged as a figure of immense popularity, attracting fascination, veneration, and also emulation. Padre Pio, who once wrote in a letter, "I am a mystery to myself," is certainly a mystery to all who know of him. To those who moved beyond mere credulity, he became an inspiration to embrace the fullness of faith. Perhaps that is why his shrine in outlying San Giovanni Rotondo, Italy, is second only to the Vatican itself in annual number of pilgrims and why Italian Catholics now report to praying more for St. Pio's intercession than for that of any other saint.

This book is a concise introduction to Padre Pio's life, especially as compared to the example and journey of his spiritual father, St. Francis of Assisi. If St. Francis is said to be the most popular saint of all time, Franciscan Capuchin Padre Pio is perhaps the most popular saint of *our* times. It is no wonder: Padre Pio miraculously bore the wounds of Jesus in his living body, prophesied the future, read the secrets of hearts, and traveled across the world in a split second. He was also a man of holy boldness, unafraid to offend in charity for the sake of truth or to call out sin for what it was. And he was a favorite of Pope St. John Paul II, who canonized him in 2002.

Given that he passed only in 1968, it is remarkable to think that such a spiritual "superhero" could exist in our modern age. How could he even survive in it? In truth, he barely did—even in the

Church. We can marvel at the depth of his involvement in the spiritual world and be reminded of it in the face of our culture of skepticism, but if we can find anything truly in common with this saint, perhaps it is the hardship and crushing misfortune that he faced in this world. He was a man of sorrows who knew how to accept God's will prayerfully even when it hurt and who, despite everything, had the courage to uplift others cheerfully by saying, "Pray, hope, and don't worry."

Through not spared from misfortune, he was spared those things that cloud us from perceiving the world in a truly spiritual way. Perhaps that is why Padre Pio offers us just the message we need to hear.

Introduction

St. Padre Pio was truly a man in the world but not of the world. It was as if St. Francis himself, called by some the most Christ-like man who ever lived, had re-emerged in our own times. Like St. Francis, the father of his order and patron saint, Padre Pio bore the stigmata—the miraculous imprint of the five wounds of Christ—in his body. Both were singularly driven by love of Christ and gave complete abandon to him. On that account, St. Francis and Padre Pio were each sharply countercultural in living a life of extreme austerity and piety. Both embraced redemptive suffering in the midst of devastating illnesses and spite from those around them. Both utterly shunned the world and its glory while being hailed as living saints by the masses during their own lifetimes. Both were surrounded by diverse, inexplicable and miraculous phenomena and had great efficacy in their prayers. Both waged dramatic battles with the spiritual forces of evil. Both had great zeal for the Eucharist and devotion to the Blessed Virgin Mary. And both were canonized as saints by the Church in a remarkably short period of time after their deaths, becoming the subject of much devotion among the faithful.

Padre Pio was guided throughout his life by the spirituality and example of St. Francis. His parents, Grazio Mario Forgione and Maria Giuseppa di Nunzio, were faithful Catholic peasants and had particular devotion to the Saint of Assisi as protector of the poor. The future Padre Pio (or Father Pio), born as Francesco Forgione in 1887, followed his baptismal namesake from a young age, even dedicating himself to St. Francis at the tender age of five. Young Francesco Forgione, who experienced a number of visions of St. Francis throughout his life, was impressed by the admirable, cheerful demeanor of a Capuchin Franciscan by the name of Fra Camillo, who often visited Francesco's hometown of Pietrelcina in southern Italy. Francesco later entered the novitiate in 1903 at Fra Camillo's monastery at Morcone, about 10 miles away, and pursued Christian perfection under the Rule of St. Francis for the rest of his life.

Though not born a saint, Padre Pio was very much morally and spiritually awake from a young age. Ordained a priest in 1910, the Capuchin friar was known for being stern and forthright in shaking the self-complacent, but when the situation warranted, he could be gentle and even playful. He rarely left his monastery, and his care for souls was primarily spiritual—interceding for his spiritual children, hearing confessions, and providing guidance for long hours each day. While always living in the midst of strong Christian communities, he lived at a time when society in general was more skeptical and when the then-unified national government of Italy was hostile to the Catholic faith. Padre Pio lived until the age of 81, suffering together with the Savior, and was canonized by Pope St. John Paul II in 2002. Despite and, indeed, because of his prayer and solitude, he could not help but catch the modern world off guard by reports of his miraculous stigmata, his numerous healings, and his knowledge of events and secret thoughts that it was impossible for him to know humanly.

This account of the life and ministry of Padre Pio considers in a special way how he lived out his vocation as a Franciscan and how he brought the spirituality of St. Francis to flesh in his times. We will follow him from his early life in Pietrecina to his formation with the Capuchin friars and his ultimate assignment to the monastery at San Giovanni Rotondo. We will see how, like St. Francis, Padre Pio offered himself as a victim to God through his many trials in life. We will also look at the many gifts that God gave him and how they built up the faith of those around him.

Understanding the Franciscan dimension of Padre Pio is important for understanding his message and spirituality since it was so important to him personally. May this immersion in the lives of St. Francis and Padre Pio challenge us beyond our comfort zone and impel us to give ourselves to Christ more completely. As St. Francis exhorted his brothers in his last days, "Let us begin to serve the Lord our God, for up until now we have made but little progress" (St. Bonaventure, *Life of St. Francis*, 4.1).

The Forgione Family

From the very beginning, Padre Pio was "not of the world." In the year of his birth, 1887, construction was underway on the Eiffel Tower in Paris, Queen Victoria celebrated her Golden Jubilee, the Statue of Liberty in New York had already welcomed immigrants to America for several months, and cities all over the world were becoming heavily industrialized. Much of this modernization was distant to the peasants of Pietrecina, a fairly remote town of 3,000 in the province of Benevento in southern Italy. They were, indeed, affected by the world's modernization, but largely in the sense of being left in its dust. But they, unlike many of the forces at work in Italy at the time, mostly held fast to their Catholic faith.

Padre Pio's father, Grazio Mario Forgione, more often called "Zi' Orazio" (Uncle Orazio) or simply "Orazio" by his fellow townspeople, was born in Pietrecina in 1860. A photographic portrait of the elderly Orazio, who lived to the age of 86, reveals a weathered visage with a broad, playful smile and a twinkle in his eye. Cheerful and well-liked, Orazio could often be spotted chatting with his friends and neighbors. He was also a good singer, which, as a young man, helped to further his popularity among the young women. Orazio's parents had arranged a marriage for him, but on his own, he went out to pursue a different young woman—Guiseppa di Nunzio—who happened to be a member of a family of higher standing. She reciprocated his feelings, and the two were married in 1881. Orazio was a peasant farmer but was fortunate enough to own the land he worked. He was prudent and always did whatever was necessary for his family to have at least the basic necessities, even when times were the toughest.

The saint's mother, Guiseppa, whom the townspeople usually called "Mama Peppa," brought much of the family's resources from her more affluent background. This included a 2.5-acre farm outside the city at Piana Romano, given by her father as a dowry. Still, her wealth and social status were only higher in relation to that of Orazio and some of the other locals; in the grand scheme of things, she too was a peasant and, like her husband, could not read or write. Mama Peppa always retained poise and an air of dignity and would often be seen wearing a white veil in accord with her family's tradition.

For the first year of their marriage, Orazio and Guiseppa lived at her parents' home before they settled down in a place of their own in an ancient neighborhood of the city. The houses of the old neighborhood in Pietrecina were joined to a twelfth-century castle called Rione Castello. It was once a fortified town but now was surrounded by the small, red and brown-roofed edifices of the city of Pietrecina. The castle was built on a cliff called the Morgione, and residents and visitors entered into the neighborhood by way of ancient portals, including the Porta Madonnella, which was adorned with a relief the Blessed Virgin, St. Anthony, and St. Michael defeating the Devil. Each year, the residents of the city would participate in festivities to honor these and other saints on their feast days. There was no running water in the neighborhood, so residents still utilized the "Pantaniello" well. The place the Forgiones called home was a rough stone house shared with another family. The Forgiones' section was called the "Cucina"—a single, large "kitchen" room adjoined by a bedroom. The Cucina was modestly but neatly furnished and had windows, beds, and a fireplace. It lacked modern luxuries, yet Padre Pio always considered it a comfortable and happy place to be. His parents' home on Vico Storto Valle (Crooked Valley Lane) was where he was born and raised and where he spent time recovering from illness during his young adulthood.

The Forgiones had to travel a few miles to the farmland they owned at Piana Romano, which was outside the city. There was no house on the property, but when farm work grew especially busy, they would sometimes sleep overnight in the shed. On that modest patch of land, the Forgiones raised sheep and grew corn and other produce. Franci, as Francesco was sometimes called, especially enjoyed eating fried peppers from the farm.

Orazio and Guiseppa had their first child in 1882, when they were both 23 years of age; they had a boy and named him Michelle after Orazio's father. Some of Franci's stories of childhood recall working or playing with his older brother. Michelle was the firstborn of several children, but unfortunately, infant mortality was high in Italy at the time because of many diseases and lack of modern medicine; the Forgiones experienced the sadness of losing several children in infancy or early childhood. In 1884, Guiseppa gave birth to a boy (not Padre Pio) christened as Francesco, but the child died within a month. The next year, Guiseppa gave birth to a girl, Amalia, but she did not survive to the age of two. Then, on May 25, 1887, the future Padre Pio was born. Having already lost a child in early infancy, they chose to have him baptized the very next day. Guiseppa asked the priest to christen him "Francesco," the name of the boy they had lost five years prior, because of the family's particular devotion to St. Francis of Assisi as the protector of the poor. Francesco was always sickly, but he would survive to a ripe old age. Franci had three younger sisters named Felicita, Pellegrina, and Grazia. Grazia later became a Brigettine sister and took the name Sister Pia after her older brother, who had already received the stigmata. Both Felicita and Pellegrina married and had children, but Felicita died of the Spanish flu at the age of 29. Thus, Francesco grew up with a sense of the fragility of life, which likely impressed on him an appreciation of human mortality and God's eternity.

All in all, the Forgiones had five surviving children. Orazio saw to it that there was always enough food on the table and that everyone's basic needs were met. Padre Pio recalls, "In my home it was difficult to find ten liras, but we were not deprived of

anything" (*Padre Pio: My Life for Each of You,* caccioppoli.com).
One hot summer day while Franci was working alongside his
father, Orazio told the boy, "I will never let you see the sun!"
(Rev. Charles Mortimer Carty, *Padre Pio: The Stigmatist,* 1).
Franci asked what this meant. The father told the boy that he
would not have to toil like this all his life; he would provide him
an education so that the devout young boy could someday
become a monk. The children of farmers often did not attend
school because of their chores; but if they did, only three years of
public grammar school was provided in the evenings. So when
Francesco's public schooling was coming to an end, Orazio
would arrange for tutors to teach his son what would be
required of a religious vocation.

However, just before the turn of the century, when the time was
becoming critical for Francesco to further his studies, the
weather and economic conditions became such that Orazio could
not support the family on their small farm. So he sailed to
America and made much more money than before to provide for
his family and for Francesco's education. Orazio would go twice
to America to send back money to the family. Nevertheless, he
would ultimately spend the rest of his life in Italy, finally passing
in 1946 at San Giovanni Rotondo.

Though he was not born a saint, it would seem that the hand of
Providence was on Padre Pio in a special way from his earliest

days. We will examine the faith of his childhood more closely in the next chapter.

Francesco's Early Graces

Like many children, Francesco was not sent to school at first because he was needed on the farm, where he tended to the sheep and helped to clear the fields, sow the seed, and do whatever else was needed. He would work alongside his father and his older brother Michelle. An injury he received once while clearing grass with a sickle left a scar on his left little finger.

Despite the hard work, Francesco loved the farm. When he became dangerously ill with typhoid fever at age 12, he said, "If I'm dying, I want to see my beloved Piana Romana once more" (C. Bernard Ruffin, *Padre Pio: The True Story*, 30). The sick boy was helped onto a donkey, and his wish to return to visit the farm was granted. When back home without anyone else around, Francesco found the hot peppers his mother had fried for the family and the farm helpers. Hot peppers were his favorite produce from the farm, so Francesco devoured them all. He went to bed sweating, but in the morning his mother found that the boy's 40-day illness had been cured.

Francesco also loved figs. Once when he and his mother were passing by a field of broccoli belonging to another farmer, Mama Peppa wanted to pick some to eat, but her son protested that it would be a sin. But a few weeks later, Francesco was passing by a grove of fig trees with ripe figs belonging to another farmer; he couldn't help himself from snacking on a few. And when his Uncle Pellegrino sent him to buy cigars, Francesco tried one on the way home. But the first puff gave him a strong aversion. He later recalled, "It felt like the ground was shaking underneath me. When I felt better, I went back to the farm and told my uncle what had happened. Instead of scolding me, he burst out laughing. Since then there's been a barrier between me and smoking" (Renzo Allegri, *Padre Pio: Man of Hope,* 15).

Francesco also enjoyed wrestling with the other boys. His friend Luigi Orlando recalls one such time: "Francesco nearly always would beat me because he was bigger than me. Once, while we were fighting, we fell and he pinned my shoulders to the ground. In the attempt to turn him and thus reverse the situation, all my efforts were in vain, and so a strong expression escaped my lips. Franci's reaction was immediate; he disengaged himself, got up and ran away all at once because he never, ever said bad words and he didn't want to hear them either" (Jim Gallagher, *Padre Pio: The Pierced Priest,* 10). In fact, as the other children started using foul language more frequently, he avoided contact with them over concern for offending God.

One might ask why this young boy was so concerned with offending God. It was because, from a young age, he was accustomed to seeing angels pointing the way to God as well as demons, in terrifying forms, seeking his spiritual demise. But he did not at first realize that others did not experience similar things; he was surprised to find out later that they typically did not.

Padre Pio later recalled first meeting his guardian angel while he was lying in his crib as an infant. But demons also manifested to him. Once, still an infant, Francesco screamed so violently that his weary father became angry and threw the child on the bed, saying, "Was a devil born in my house instead of a Christian?" (Allegri, 11). But little Francesco slipped from the bed and hit the hard, bare floor. Mamma Peppa was terrified and screamed to her husband, "You killed my son!" Thankfully, the boy was all right, but decades later, at his father Orazio's funeral, Padre Pio recalled, "From that day on I didn't cry anymore" (*My Life for Each of You*, ch. 1). Even though Francesco was but an infant when it happened, Padre Pio was able to remember it years later and to identify the devil as the source of his childhood terrors.

Children are often afraid of monsters in the bedroom when it's dark, but for Francesco the monsters in his bedroom were real. He later shared, "My mother would turn off the lights, and so many monsters would close in on me that I would cry. She would turn the lights on and I would quiet down because the monsters vanished" (Allegri, 12). This, however, made Francesco see sin for what it was, so the boy had a particular aversion to it.

From the age of three, Francesco would recite memorized prayers. From the age of five, angels and saints were a common sight to the boy. It was during this time that he consecrated his life to God through St. Francis, who appeared to him. At nine, young Francesco would scourge himself as a penance and would leave his comfortable bed to sleep on the floor with a rock as his pillow, although his mother and the local parish priest would scold him for this unusual behavior.

When Francesco was 10 years old, his father took him by donkey on a 16-mile journey to the shrine of St. Pellegrino. After some time of prayer at the shrine, Orazio was ready to make the journey home, but Francesco insisted on staying. While praying in the shrine, the boy's attention was drawn to a mother holding a deformed child in her arms. For a long time, the woman prayed desperately for the child to be healed, and Francesco, as he watched, also pleaded with God to do something. At last, the woman thrust the child on the altar and cried out, "If you won't cure him, you can keep him then. Here, he's yours" (Gallagher, 12). At once the child was miraculously healed, and Francesco would remember that moment for the rest of his life.

Realizing His Vocation

Desiring to rely on nothing but the Lord, St. Francis followed Jesus' counsel in the Gospel to his disciples when he sent them out to preach: "Take nothing for the journey, neither walking staff nor traveling bag; no bread, no money. No one is to have two coats" (Lk. 9:3). Francis and his "lesser brothers" vowed to a life of holy poverty so that their hearts would be fixed only on God and they would look only to the Holy Spirit, rather than to human effort, for their needs. Throughout the centuries and as their ranks grew, the strict observance of poverty was a challenge to St. Francis' followers, the Franciscans. Thus, in the sixteenth century, a reform movement emerged to restore a strict observance of the rule as lived by Francis himself. These Franciscans came to be called "Capuchins" after the color of their dusty brown, hooded habits.

The Capuchins had a monastery about 14 miles northwest of Pietrecina at Morcone. The friars there, holding to the strict observance of poverty, not only held everything in common but even refrained from storing provisions for more than a few days. Instead, a brother was sent to go about and beg for provisions for the community, and the job even had a special name: *cercatore di campagna* (country gatherer). Twenty-six-year-old Fra Camillo was one such friar. He would go about the region collecting provisions and would also make spiritual contact with those in the surrounding areas. The children loved Fra Camillo, who gave them treats and attention, and Francesco got to know him well. Fra Camillo stopped by the farm, and the 10-year-old Francesco was much impressed with him and with his stories about the life of St. Francis, the boy's patron saint and the charismatic founder of the friar's order. The friar, with his thick and billowing beard, struck a chord with Francesco, who from then on wanted to be nothing else but "a friar with a beard like Fra Camillo" (*My Life...* ch. 1). Much to young Francesco's delight, the friar told him that all Capuchins wear beards. The constitution of the Capuchin Franciscans at the time required the friars to wear one after the custom of St. Francis.

Realizing his interest in the Capuchins, Francesco's parents took him to Morcone to visit the monastery. The boy wanted to know if they "wanted him"; he was delighted to find that they did, and he jumped for joy. But his parents also found out from the friars that Francesco would need more schooling. Only three years of public schooling was offered. To further his studies, Francesco would need either to enroll in a private school or to find a tutor. He ended up doing a combination of both. Much of the time, he was tutored since he was still needed in the fields. Even so, the Forgiones could not afford this, especially given the poor harvest during that time and lack of employment opportunities outside of farming. Therefore, Orazio decided, as did many other Italian men at the time, to go to America for a while to find work. He would keep his promise to his son to provide for him to become a monk. After first sailing to South America but not finding gainful employment, Orazio returned and then set sail for New York City. He found a job working on a farm in New Castle, Pennsylvania, and was promoted to foreman. Thanks to this job, he was able to send home enough money to pay for Francesco's education and to purchase two farms and some livestock back home. Orazio continued working in America for several years, possibly from 1897 to 1903, while returning home periodically for visits. Francesco's older brother Michelle, who had already found that school was not for him, joined his father for a time working in America.

In 1889, at the age of 12, Francesco received the sacrament of Confirmation in his home parish of Our Lady of the Angels in Pietrecina. His father could not attend since he was working in America. Not long afterward, Francesco received his first Holy Communion. Francesco longed to receive Jesus in this sacrament, but the priest insisted that even though Francesco was thoroughly prepared, he must wait until the usual time to receive Communion with the other children.

Francesco had a number of teachers and tutors throughout his private education since the choices for the Forgiones were limited. His first two tutors had only received a basic education themselves and, thus, could only take him so far. After this, Francesco began studies in reading, writing, and Latin at a school run by Don Domenico Tizzani, a former priest who was then married. Francesco did not excel under Don Domenica, and the fact that he had left the priesthood bothered the Forgiones, so they pulled Francesco out of that school. Next, he studied under a known professional teacher named Don Angelo Caccavo, earning his elementary and secondary diplomas. Finally, Francesco began to thrive academically, even rising to the top of the class. Under Don Angelo, the boy wrote a number of excellent essays and creative pieces, including the following essay, entitled "If I Were King":

> O, if I were king! How many wonderful things I would wish to do. First of all, I would always want to be a religious king, as I am now and as I always hope to be. I would fight, first of all, against divorce, which so many wicked men desire, and make people respect as much as possible the sacrament of matrimony.
>
> What happened to Julian the Apostate, who was brave, self-controlled, and studious, but who made the big mistake of denying Christianity, in which he was educated, because he decided to revive Paganism? His life was wasted because he did not attain anything but the despicable name of apostate.
>
> Also, I would try to make a name for myself by always fighting for the path of true Christianity. Woe to the person who does not wish to follow it! ... My motto would be the same as Alessandro Severo's: "Don't do unto others

that which you would not want them to do to you." During my reign I would spend all my time visiting the provinces in order to improve the government there, and by building everywhere some distinguished monuments as memorials, such as city gates, roads, circuses, libraries, statues, theaters, etc. I would be gracious, humane, and observe the laws; I would travel as a simple citizen, giving audiences to everyone and dressing simply by wearing clothing made by the women back home. I would gather in my court the greatest writers. I would pay teachers of rhetoric well. I would be a patron of the arts. My motto would be that of Vespasiano; "Only a friend of mankind is worthy to lead." (Allegri, 18–19)

Francesco was always fond of the scholarly Don Angelo and had great respect for him, even though he was known to exact corporal punishment on lazy or misbehaving students. Once, the other boys framed the teenage Francesco in some misbehavior that got him a share of this punishment. They wrote a passionate and inappropriate love letter to a girl and signed it with Francesco's name, even though Francesco himself would shrink at the very thought of any indecency. The girl was aghast and turned the letter into the teacher, who pummeled poor Francesco in front of the classroom, leaving him with bruises for days. The prank was later discovered, and the teacher was deeply sorry for his rash judgment.

Francesco and Don Angelo stayed in touch. Though he had spent some time in seminary, Don Angelo was no longer a religious man, so Francesco—later Padre Pio—would often pray for his conversion. His former teacher did return to the faith and visited Padre Pio numerous times at San Giovanni Rotondo.

Preparing for Spiritual Battle

In 1902, Francesco was about to enter the Capuchin novitiate, a period of formal discernment and formation, within the monastery at Morcone, but one of his classmates had another trick up his sleeve to make sport of the boy's innocence. Francesco was a devoted altar boy at his parish church, Our Lady of the Angels, but suddenly the archpriest, Don Salvatore Pannullo, had him removed from service (Gallagher, 20). The cleric had received an anonymous letter accusing Francesco of having sexual relations with a girl in town—an accusation that could block his entry into the Capuchins. Padre Pio later recalled that, although then in his teens, he did not even know at the time about the "birds and the bees," let alone engage in fornication. Indeed, Francesco was naively unaware that his being removed from serving had anything to do with allegations of misconduct. Fortunately, Don Pannullo, who was a friend and mentor to Francesco, looked into the matter and found the sender of the anonymous letter, who admitted to fabricating the false charge. Francesco was cleared of the accusation, but he had further struggles in making entry into the Capuchins.

Though Francesco had a burning desire to serve God and become a "priest with a beard," the sensitive youth of 15 had some natural apprehension about entering the austere life of the monastery, where his contact with family and friends would be sharply limited and he would forgo the simple comforts of home and familiar surroundings. However, in 1903, Francesco experienced a vision that gave him encouragement and challenge in going forward in his vocation. Writing of himself in the third person, Francesco wrote of the vision:

> At his side he beheld a majestic man of rare beauty, resplendent as the sun. This man took him by the hand and said, "Come with me, for you must fight a doughty warrior." He then let him to a vast field where there was a great multitude. The multitude was divided into two groups. On the one side, he saw men of most beautiful countenance, clad in snow-white garments. On the other ... he saw men of most hideous aspect, dressed in black raiment like so many dark shadows.

> Between these great groups of people was a great space in which that soul was placed by his guide. As he gazed intently and with wonder... in the midst of the space that divided the two groups, a man appeared, advancing so tall that his very forehead seem to touch the heavens, while his face ... horrible it was.

> At this point the poor soul was so completely disconcerted that he felt that his life was suspended. The strange personage approach nearer and nearer, and the guide who was beside the soul informed him that he would have to fight with that creature. At these words the poor little soul turned pale, trembled all over and was

about to fall to the ground in a faint, so great was his fear.

The guide supported him with one arm until he recovered somewhat from his fright. The soul then turned to his guide and begged him to spare him from the fury of that eerie personage, because he said that the man was so strong that the strength of all men combined would not be sufficient to fell him.

"Your every resistance is in vain. You must fight with this man. Take heart. Enter the combat with confidence. Go forth courageously. I shall be with you. In reward for your victory over him I will give you a shining crown to adorn your brow."

The poor little soul took heart. He entered into combat with the formidable and mysterious being. The attack [of the giant] was ferocious, but with the help of his guide, who never left his side, [the soul] finally overcame his adversary, threw him to the ground, and forced him to flee.

Then his guide, faithful to his promise, took from beneath his robes a crown of rarest beauty, a beauty that words cannot describe, and placed it on his head. Then he withdrew it again, saying, "I will reserve for you a crown even more beautiful if you fight the good fight with the being whom you have just fought. He will continually renew the assault to regain his lost honor. Fight valiantly and do not doubt my aide. Keep your eyes wide open, for that mysterious personage will try to take you by surprise. Do not fear his ... formidable might, but remember what I have promised you: that I will always be close at hand and I will always help you, so that you will always succeed in conquering him."

When that mysterious man had been vanquished, all the multitude of men of horrible countenance took to flight with shrieks, curses, and deafening cries, while from the other multitude of men came the sound of applause and praise for the splendid man, more radiant than the sun, who had assisted the poor soul so splendidly in the fierce battle. And so the vision ended (Ruffin, 40–41).

Francesco had already become familiar with the spiritual world of angels and demons and the war between them with souls hanging in the balance. But in that moment, he realized anew that his part in the battle was great, that the crown was worth the great sacrifices that lie ahead, and that God would be ever with him.

Entry into the Monastery

On January 6, 1903, at the age of 15, Francesco Forgione set out for the Capuchin monastery in Morcone, making the journey by donkey and by train. Giving him a Rosary, his mother said goodbye to him with these words: "My heart is bleeding, but St. Francis has called you and you must go" (Gallagher, 23). His mother then charged him to pray many Rosaries. The boy was accompanied by the local priest Don Nicola Caruso, by his teacher Don Angelo Caccavo, and by two other boys from Pietrecina seeking entrance into the monastery. They did not need to bring their things or any clothes; their new life was one of holy poverty with all things held in common. In fact, upon entering the monastery, even their travel clothes would be ceremonially removed and replaced with the brown habit of the Capuchins.

The monastery at Morcone offered a sweeping view of the Italian countryside. The courtyard was dotted with palm trees, and the grounds were surrounded by fields farmed by the friars. When the group of travelers knocked on the door of the monastery, it was none other than Fra Camillo who answered, expressing great joy at Francesco's coming to join in communal life: "Bravo, Franci, bravo. You've been faithful to the calling and promise of St. Francis. Bravo, Franci" (Gallagher, 24). Then the boys took an academic examination, and Francesco passed, much to Don Angelo's pleasure. One of the boys was not old enough the enter novitiate since he had not yet turned 15, so he returned with the priest and the teacher on the journey back to Pietrecina until he could enter.

The other two boys were clothed in the habit of the Capuchins for the novitiate year of discernment. The ceremony emphasized the break with their old life and the dawn of the new—a ritual clearly reminiscent of, and building upon, that of baptism. As his old coat was removed, Francesco heard the words, "May the Lord strip you of the old man," and as he was dressed in the brown habit of the Capuchins, "May the Lord clothe you in the new man" (*My Life...* ch. 2). He was also prepared for combat with the devil: "May the Lord put the hood of salvation upon your head, to defeat the deceptions of the devil." The young man was given a cord around his waist that held up the baggy brown robe: "May the Lord gird you with the cordon of purity and extinguish the fire of lust so that the virtues of continence and chastity might abide in you." Finally, he was given a new name: The superior, Padre Tommaso, gave him the name Pio of Pietrecina, probably after the martyr Pope St. Pius I (d. 154), whose relics were kept at Pietrecina.

The stories of St. Francis to which Fra Camillo had introduced him likely flashed through Brother Pio's mind in those first days at the monastery. Perhaps he recalled the story of how St. Francis renounced all his earthly possessions, even the very clothes off his back. The young St. Francis, after his conversion, was moved by charity and zeal to give as much as he could to the poor—but this included clothing from his father's merchandise and money from his father. So his father, the merchant Pietro Bernadone, after having his son locked in his dungeon for some time, hauled him before the bishop of Assisi to have him disinherited. Francis removed even the clothing off his back and returned it to his raging father, saying, "Hitherto I have called thee my father on earth, but henceforth I can confidently say 'Our Father, Which art in heaven,' with Whom I have laid up my whole treasure, and on Whom I have set my whole trust and hope" (St. Bonaventure, 2.3).

Or perhaps Brother Pio remembered how St. Francis, when tempted in his younger days by lustful thoughts, would not spare himself from extreme penances but would scourge himself and throw himself bloodied and naked onto a snow bank in the cold of winter. The Saint of Assisi was always careful to keep his body, which he called "Brother Ass," in line. St. Bonaventure, his biographer, wrote, "Of his drinking of wine what shall I say, when even of water he would scarce drink what he needed, while parched with burning thirst? He was always discovering methods of more rigorous abstinence, and would daily make progress in their use, and albeit he had already attained the summit of perfection, yet, like a novice, he was ever making trial of some new method, chastising the lusts of the flesh by afflicting it" (5.1).

Brother Pio would need to remember such stories since the trials of the novitiate would be rigorous indeed. Renzo Allegri, a biographer of Padre Pio, describes the austerity of life in the monastery at Morcone:

> Padre Pio occupied cell number 28. His bed consisted of a wood frame with a mattress full of corn husks. The novice was expected to go to bed fully clothed. He would take off only his sandals, and he would carefully arrange the fabric of his habit on top of him so that it would not become wrinkled. He was required to sleep flat on his back without moving, with his arms in the form of a cross over his chest and with a large crucifix stuck in his belt.
>
> At midnight his sleep was suddenly interrupted by the sound of a bell. All the monks rose quickly and gathered together in the church to recite matins and lauds. Waking up in the middle of the night, when the body was just beginning to savor sleep's restorative benefits, was an extremely harsh penance. These prayers lasted more than an hour, and when the monks went back to bed they often could not fall asleep. In winter, though, this practice was truly torture. The damp cold of the corridors and of the church penetrated the bones of the monks and made them shiver. No Capuchin friar ever grew accustomed to this penitential practice, so one can imagine how difficult it was for a sixteen-year-old boy.

The monks then awoke at five o'clock in the morning to begin the day's activities. The novice was expected to make his bed, put a wooden crucifix on top of the mattress, and hurry to the church once again. The friars moved from one place to another as a community: the novices had to observe complete silence as they walked in a straight line with their eyes looking down. They were punished for even the slightest failure to do so. (27–28)

Punishment was severe. Padre Tommaso, the superior of the monastery, would often whip the backs of the novices until they bled. Everyone was a sinner, so all the friars scourged themselves once a week together at night in the unlit chapel. Brother Pio, however, was rarely in need of punishment for disobedience. He later recalled, "If my superior ordered me to jump out of the window, I would not argue. I would jump." Only meager meals were served. Novices were not allowed to eat until the superior gave them his blessing, for which they would have to kneel down and ask. Sometimes the superior would decline the blessing, and the novices would have to remain kneeling for the entire meal while the others ate. The other boy who entered the monastery together with Brother Pio left within two months, saying, "Back home we pay a dime to see madmen. Here we see them for free" (*My Life…* ch. 2). Still, there was a "method to the madness" for those who would submit to it.

The Capuchins

The Capuchins, or Order of Friars Minor Capuchin, were the strictest order of Franciscans. Even by the time of Francis' death in 1226, the Franciscans numbered in the thousands. Three centuries later, with the order's numbers swollen even further, living the Franciscan ideal of strict poverty and penance became more of a challenge, and laxity and power politics also contributed to tepidity among some Franciscans. Fra Matteo Serafini of Bascio, a sixteenth-century Franciscan, wanted to return to the Franciscan ideal but came into conflict with his superiors, who sought to have him arrested and put in jail. He fled in 1520 to a Camaldolese monastery for refuge and, in 1528, was given the blessing of Pope Clement VII to live out the Franciscan ideal together with those who might wish to join him. The name "Capuchin" was popularly given to them because of the dusty brown color of the habit they adopted from the Camaldolese monks who had taken in their founder.

Fra Matteo and his companions followed the Rule of St. Francis to the letter and devised a constitution to guard the strict interpretation of the Rule. In the Capuchin Constitutions of 1536, we read, "It was not only the will of our Father Saint Francis but also that of Christ our redeemer for the Rule to be observed simply, to the letter and without gloss just as our first seraphic Fathers observed it. Since our Rule is very clear, and so that it may be observed more purely, spiritually and in a holy manner, all glosses and fleshly, useless and compromising explanations are rejected. These uproot the Rule from the pious, just and holy mind of our Lord Christ who spoke in Saint Francis" (trans. by Paul Hanbridge).

One might ask what exactly the Rule of St. Francis is. Many founders of religious orders throughout history have written 'rules' to direct the community life for future generations to their spiritual end and their particular 'charism,' or gift. Francis' Rule has been described as getting to the heart of the counsels of Christ in the Gospel in such a way as Francis himself was given to live out in his own Christ-like life. The Rule is only a few pages long. It begins in this way: "The Rule and life of the Friars Minor is this, namely, to observe the Holy Gospel of our Lord Jesus Christ by living in obedience, without property, and in chastity" (1).

The Rule further provides guidelines for admitting new friars, taking Jesus' counsel in the Matthew's Gospel as the guiding principle: "they should go and sell all that belongs to them and endeavour to give it to the poor" (2). The Rule directs for poverty to be internalized, advising that friars wear poor and rough clothing, wear shoes only in true necessity, and only ride on horseback if they are too ill to walk. But while insisting on strict penance, it also condemns judgment of others. St. Francis wrote, "I warn all the friars and exhort them not to condemn or look down on people whom they see wearing soft or gaudy clothes and enjoying luxuries in food or drink; each one should rather condemn and despise himself" (2).

St. Francis also exhorted, "And this is my advice, my counsel, and my earnest plea to my friars in our Lord Jesus Christ that, when they travel about the world, they should not be quarrelsome or take part in disputes with words or criticize others; but they should be gentle, peaceful, and unassuming, courteous and humble, speaking respectfully to everyone, as is expected of them" (3). The Rule forbids friars from owning anything or from taking money. "I strictly forbid all the friars to accept money in any form, either personally or through an intermediary. The ministers and superiors, however, are bound to provide carefully for the needs of the sick and the clothing of the other friars, by having recourse to spiritual friends, while taking into account differences of place, season, or severe climate, as seems best to them in the circumstances. This does not dispense them from the prohibition of receiving money in any form" (4). Finally, the Rule provided direction on prayer, work, discipline, ministry, and the governance of the order. Notably, St. Francis designated that the leader of the order be called 'minister general' in order to remind them of Christ's teaching that the greatest is the one who serves.

During the novitiate year, Brother Pio was not allowed to read any books apart from 15 pages of assigned spiritual reading for the entire year. St. Francis at first thought that learning tended to cloud the pure light of Gospel simplicity in one's life. St. Bonaventure's humble study of theology, however, showed him that it is possible for scholars, too, to be childlike. Still, Brother Pio's superior thought it best for the novices to realize that their focus is prayer and not academic learning or worldly curiosity, even though they would have to complete several years of study after their novitiate had ended in formation for the priesthood. In the Capuchin Constitutions of 1536, we read, "The friars should also always try to speak about God as this may truly help them to be kindled in His love and so that the Gospel teaching may bear fruit in our hearts. To uproot any Darnel that might suffocate this, we direct that none of our places should have, for any reason at all, fatuous or vain books, so harmful to the spirit of Christ our Lord and God" (1). Brother Pio, however, found the prohibition on reading difficult since, during that time, he lost a lot of ground in his literacy, which had to be regained later.

The friars had their clothing in common, which meant that the habits did not always fit. This, too, goes back to the Capuchin Constitutions: "It was not without reason that Jesus commended the austerity of Saint John the Baptist's clothing when He said that those who dress in fine clothes are in the houses of Kings. Therefore we instruct the friars, who have chosen to be abject in the house of God, to dress in the poorest, roughest, most abject, austere and worthless cloth readily found in the provinces where they are" (2). Likewise, Brother Pio's bed of straw was not out of a lack of materials but an implementation of the Capuchin Constitutions: "we direct the friars, unless already infirm or very weak, not to sleep on anything except bare boards, mats, broom, ferns or on a little straw or hay. Let them not sleep on blankets" (2).

Novices were further forbidden from making eye contact and from showing affection. This was intended to foster humility and detachment from excessive and selfish loves. So after almost a year apart, when his mother was allowed to come visit him, Brother Pio felt the need to follow what was prescribed him. His mother was horrified by this behavior and wanted to take him home right then; he was so thin and would not even accept the candies she had made especially for him. Padre Pio later recalled how very much he wanted to embrace her in that moment, but he could not because he was under obedience.

These disciplines, however, did bear spiritual fruit in Brother Pio's life. His prayer life was so moving and intense that he was often found sobbing while meditating in the chapel. Also, when another novice entered the monastery just a few months after Brother Pio, Brother Pio was assigned to give him some instruction. Brother Angelico da Sarno later recalled, "For three months, Pio every day explained to me the rules and

constitutions. Every day I was longing for this encounter. He was only few months older than me" (*My Life...* ch. 2).

Suffering in Body and Soul

After the novitiate year was completed, Brother Pio made his temporary vows of poverty, chastity, and obedience for a three-year period of formal discernment and study. Not long prior, his father had come to the monastery to straighten out the situation and possibly bring his Francesco home to Pietrecina, but the superiors assured him that everything was all right and that his son's aloofness during his mother's visit was not a sign of madness but simply obedience to the discipline required of him in the novitiate. Brother Pio's mother returned to Morcone in January 1904 for the ceremony in which he would make his temporary vows. Mamma Peppa was proud of her son and was happy for him, telling him, "My son, now you really are a son of Saint Francis. May he bless you!" (*My Life...* ch. 2).

The program called for another six years of study for the priesthood. Brother Pio was assigned to study at the seminary at Sant'Elia a Pianisi, over 20 miles northeast of Morcone and 30 miles north of Pietrecina, but it was there that greater trials would begin. Brother Pio started to become subject to a debilitating illness, possibly the result of demonic attacks. Doctors at the time were unable to diagnose it. Often Brother Pio would be sent home to Pietrecina to recover only for the illness to vanish upon his arrival; this was a state of affairs some of the other brothers thought simply too convenient, especially given that the seminarians were allowed only a few short absences during their formation. But on one such trip, suffering in a particular way from his chronic stomach ailments, headaches, fever, sweats, cough, and chest pains, young Brother Pio was so ill that he had to stop every few minutes to regain his strength to go on.

Meanwhile, the devil's visible manifestations to Brother Pio intensified while he was at Sant'Elia a Pianisi. One night, poor Brother Pio could not sleep. He thought he heard footsteps in the next cell and had a mind to chat with the other brother, who he thought must also be suffering from insomnia. Brother Pio stepped to his window to look toward his neighbor's, but what he saw was not another brother but a huge and raging black dog with violent eyes crouching on the window ledge of the other cell. The next day, upon asking other brothers about that cell, he found out that it had been a month since anyone had occupied it. Oftentimes, the devil would even physically assault Brother Pio in the night, leaving him with bruises.

Perhaps on such occasions Brother Pio thought of the struggles his spiritual father St. Francis had with the devil. St. Bonaventure recounted a story of how, one night, the devil assaulted St. Francis with a very severe headache (5.3). As a penance, the saint typically refused to sleep on a pillow, but that night he accepted one because of his illness. However, all night St. Francis' thoughts were very distracted, and he could not pray. Perceiving the work of the devil in this, he asked one of the brothers to take the pillow far away from him since the devil was using it. But after the brother had left, as he was carrying the pillow, the devil attacked the brother, immobilizing him completely. In his mind's eye, St. Francis was given to see the brother's plight, and he cast off the devil and his tricks.

On account of his illness, Brother Pio was reassigned a number of times. In the summer of 1905, he was sent to the Abbey of Santa Maria del Monte, closer to the coast of the Adriatic Sea, with hopes for his convalescence. But seeing that this was of no avail, his superiors sent him later that year to the seminary at San Marco la Catola, in a mountainous region not far from Sant'Elia a Pianisi, to study philosophy. In 1907, Brother Pio made his solemn vows in the Capuchin Order. Because of his illness, however, Brother Pio was allowed to return to Pietrecina again for an extended period of time and to receive theological instruction from the local priest.

Brother Pio received minor orders in Pietrecina from the bishop in late 1908. At the time, men nearing the end of their formation for the priesthood would be admitted into the first rank of the Church's hierarchy by being given the 'minor orders' of porter, exorcist, lector, and acolyte. As porter, Brother Pio would have been given the duty of tending to the doors of the church; as exorcist, he would have been given authority over the devil; as lector, he would have read the Scriptures in church; and as acolyte, he would have been given particular duties in serving at the altar. After the Second Vatican Council, the Church no longer conferred the orders of porter and exorcist as part of the steps to priestly ordination but continued to confer the 'ministries' of lector and acolyte.

The following year was the time for the next step toward the priesthood—being ordained a deacon, the first of the major orders—in which Brother Pio would be enabled to read the Gospel in church, to perform baptisms and weddings, and to distribute Holy Communion. But because of his ill health, he was not well prepared for the required theological examination. Having denied waiving the exam because of Brother Pio's poor health, the archbishop of Benevento determined to see for himself what theological knowledge Brother Pio had. After meeting with Brother Pio in Benevento and testing him, the archbishop approved for him to be ordained a deacon. So they set out for Morcone, where he ordained Brother Pio a deacon in the presence of his Capuchin brethren.

Again, however, Deacon Pio's health took a turn to the worse, so much so that he was not even certain whether he would live to see his priestly ordination and celebrate his first Mass as he so desired. He was in intense pain yet so aware of the redemptive value of his suffering that he did not despise death but, rather, only wished that he could be ordained a priest first. The only issue was that he was not yet 24, which was the minimum age at the time for priestly ordination. For this, the archbishop was willing to give a dispensation, and Deacon Pio was ordained a priest at the cathedral at Benevento in 1910 at the age of 23. He journeyed back to Pietrecina to celebrate his first Mass at his home parish of Our Lady of the Angels four days later.

Supernatural Gifts at Pietrecina

Already in 1908, a few years before his priestly ordination, Pio's supernatural gifts were being awakened. His aunt Daria suffered serious burns on her face from a freak accident. She was holding a lantern to cast some light for herself while looking for something in her shed in Pietrecina when she got too close to her husband's gunpowder, causing an explosion that injured her badly. Desperate for some relief from the burns, she covered her face with Pio's sack that he used to use for collecting chestnuts. Miraculously, the burns on her face were completely healed (*My Life...* ch. 2).

After his priestly ordination, Padre Pio spent six years in Pietrecina to recover from his illnesses. Every morning, he would say Mass at Our Lady of the Angels Church. Already his Masses were known to last as long as three hours because of his great devotion to the Eucharist. Then he would head out to his family's farm at Piana Romana. It was about a half hour by foot, but Padre Pio would stop to rest along the way, and he was often seen shielding himself from the sun with his umbrella. During his stay in Pietrecina, he spent much of his time building spiritual friendships with people, who would remember their encounter with him for a long time after.

The people of Pietrecina came to know him as a holy man and sought him out for prayer and advice. Once, the local farmers' livelihood was being decimated by a plague of lice. The farmers went to Padre Pio, asking for his prayers. He walked with them through the fields, and as he prayed, the farmers could hear the lifeless insects falling off the crops and to the ground (Allegri, 42).

Padre Pio was accustomed to take evening walks with Don Pannullo, the pastor at Our Lady of the Angels and a good friend of his for many years. Once when they heard the bells of the church, which would ring out at regular intervals, Padre Pio prophesied that in the countryside where the echo of the bell could be heard, there would one day be a monastery of Capuchins with monks chanting their prayers. This prediction would be brought about in the late 1940s by one of Padre Pio's spiritual daughters, Maria Pyle, a wealthy American who gave away her money and spent her years helping with Padre Pio's apostolates.

At Pietrecina, Padre Pio's battle with the devil intensified. The attacks would take place at night when Padre Pio was alone in his room. Crashing noises could be heard even from far away, and the townspeople knew what was going on. Demons would appear in bodily form and would fling themselves onto poor Padre Pio, even causing him physical injury so that he could not sleep. Padre Pio would emerge in the morning drenched in sweat, bruised and bloodied, with his room in shambles from the demons throwing the furniture about. He wrote to his spiritual director about these phenomena, but sometimes the demons would try to prevent him from reading the letters that came in reply. Padre Pio would open up the envelope only to find a blank page inside, or there would be ink spilt over the words, rendering them illegible. Still, he knew that these tricks could be overcome by prayer. He sprinkled holy water over the letter and illegible parts became legible. Another time, his spiritual director wrote a letter to Padre Pio in Greek to see if these would make a difference. Even though Padre Pio had never learned Greek, he was able to understand the contents of the letter. He explained, "My guardian angel explained everything to me" (Allegri, 45).

Padre Pio had always had a deep prayer life. He wrote to a spiritual director about his life of prayer:

> The usual way of my prayer is this. As soon as I open myself to prayer, the soul begins to gather in peace and tranquility which is not possible to express in words. The senses are suspended, except for hearing, which sometimes is not suspended, but this usually does not bother me and I must say that even if there is much sound around me, it doesn't bother me at all. From here you'll see that sometimes I can converse with the intellect. Often it happens to me that when I think of God, who is always present to me, I move away a bit from the mind, then I feel a stretch in touch from our Lord in a very penetrating and sweet manner in the center of the soul in

which, more often than not, I am forced to shed tears of sorrow for my infidelity and tenderness to have a father so good and so attentive to call me to his presence. At other times it happens to me that I am in a great aridity of spirit; I feel my body in a great oppression from many infirmities, I feel that it is impossible to gather myself and pray, and how much I wish I had. This state of affairs is increasingly intensified, that if I do not die, it is a miracle of the Lord (Epist. I, 420 s.).

Several times, Padre Pio asked God to allow him to suffer for the salvation of souls. In 1910, only a few weeks after his priestly ordination, Padre Pio was praying at Piana Romana when Jesus and Mary appeared to him and gave him the wounds of Christ on his hands and feet. It started with only penny-sized red areas on the palms of his hands and on his feet, accompanied by sharp pains. Though perhaps baffled that it could happen to him, Padre Pio certainly knew about the stigmata of St. Francis and a number of other saints who bore the wounds of Christ in their flesh. Though pleased to suffer for Christ, he also knew that there would be trouble once it became widely known that he had these sacred wounds: people would venerate him as a saint, which might become a temptation to pride; the religious authorities might become suspicious of him as a spiritual charlatan trying to make himself look holy; and other religious might become jealous of his favor with God. So Padre Pio confided his secret to

Don Pannullo, a man he could trust. The two of them prayed, and the outward signs of the stigmata vanished though the pain continued. Still, when the time was right a few years later, God would make the stigmata visible again for all to see, and Padre Pio would have to suffer the consequences.

Meanwhile, monks were already becoming jealous of Padre Pio's earthly privileges. They felt he was allowed to stay away from the monastery in his hometown for too long, and they even felt that he was trying to contrive the situation to suit his own comforts. Concerned, perhaps, about the friars' sentiments on the matter, Padre Pio's superior Padre Benedetto ordered him back to the monastery. Yet it had become clear from Padre Pio's many years of illness that Pietrecina was the only place where he could at least hold down a little nourishment. Everywhere else Padre Pio went, he had to be sent home since he could hold nothing down for more than 15 minutes. It seemed that, for some mysterious reason, Pietrecina was the only place Padre Pio could survive. Padre Pio wrote in a letter during that time, "It's true that at home I have suffered and am suffering, but I've never been unable to fulfill my duties, which has not been the case in the monastery" (Allegri, 49–50). Furthermore, five times Padre Benedetto had ordered Padre Pio back to the monastery, but each time he became violently ill and unable to go. Finally, Fr. Benedetto insisted that the young friar return to the monastery—that if it be God's will for him to die there, so be it.

Padre Pio protested for the sake of his life but also realized that, on account of his vows, he was strictly bound to obedience.

A Time of Trial and Transition

Before submitting to such an order, which he believed would be detrimental to his health, Padre Pio asked for permission to be examined by a medial specialist. Padre Benedetto granted him his request and sent him to be examined by Dr. Antonio Cardarelli, a prestigious physician, in Naples. The year was 1911, and Padre Pio was 24 years old. Dr. Cardarelli's prognosis gave Padre Pio only one month to live, and he advised the friars to take him to a nearby monastery to spend his final days. The friars took him to the monastery of Venafro.

At Venafro, Padre Pio was too weak to join in the communal prayer of the monastery; but confined to his bed, he would experience hours of ecstasies in which he would speak with heavenly beings and then would be subject to periods of demonic appearances and abuse (Ruffin, 84–85). His ecstasies would often last about two hours, during which he would not even respond to a light being shined into his face. The demonic attacks were much shorter, but they were extremely violent and would often leave Padre Pio physically injured. Friars elsewhere in the monastery were terrified by the violent crashing noises that emerged from the bedridden priest's cell. One friar went to visit Padre Pio to see for himself what was going on. Padre Pio told him that maybe the devil wouldn't come that night. Nothing happened, so the friar left. But he only had taken a few steps out of the cell when there was a huge crashing noise. The friar bolted back to see if Padre Pio was all right. The demons would only attack when Padre Pio was alone. But despite his intense spiritual experiences at Venafro, Padre Pio's health remained stable. In fact, he became well enough to be sent home again to Pietrecina, where he remained for several years.

Meanwhile, his superiors sought to have the archbishop of Benevento secularize Padre Pio, that is, to remove him from the Capuchin order and make him a diocesan priest. While he was still at Venafro, he pleaded with St. Francis, who appeared to him, "My father, are you chasing me away from your Order? Let me die, instead" (*My Life...* ch. 3). As it happened, the archbishop denied the appeal for his secularization, and the Vatican gave special permission for Padre Pio to live as a Capuchin outside of community until his health should improve.

But then Padre Pio was drafted into the Italian military at the dawn of the First World War in 1915, since every able-bodied male was needed. Though he was hardly able-bodied, the military doctors were not at all hasty in releasing him from duty. They detained him for some time at Benevento and then sent him on to Naples, where he was assigned to the medical corps. Finally, a military doctor at Naples diagnosed him in December 1915 with pulmonary infiltration before he was admitted for service and sent him home for six months, after which he was to await further orders.

Padre Pio had developed a correspondence with a pious visionary named Raffaellina Cerase, an elderly noblewoman. After she became ill and was nearing death, she notified Padre Pio's superiors so they could send him to her. The superiors saw an opportunity in this since there was a Capuchin monastery in Foggia, where the noblewoman lay ill. They wanted to make sure that Padre Pio would live within Capuchin community and away from his family. They gave Padre Pio permission to visit his friend in Foggia, and when he arrived he found that Padre Benedetto had given him the order, "Stay forever in Foggia, whether dead or alive" (Allegri, 58). So Padre Pio remained in Foggia. Every day until she died, he tended to Raffaellina. Padre Pio and Raffaellina had much to share on the spiritual life. In fact, the case for her sainthood has been opened, and she is known in the Church by the title of 'Servant of God.' Meanwhile, the demons followed Padre Pio to Foggia, and other friars there testified to the strange phenomena.

It seems that people were always offering Padre Pio advice on which climate might do best for his health. A lady named Rachelina Russo, who used to tend to the needs of the friars, recommended he try the air of San Giovanni Rotondo, where there was a Capuchin monastery that had been recently reestablished and where the lady owned a store. It was known to be a backwater place, high in crime because of the poverty and pestered by gangs of thugs, so Padre Pio was at first a little apprehensive. Rachelina, however, persuaded him, saying, "Especially because we are bandits you must come. You must come and convert us" (*My Life...* ch. 4). So he went for a short visit.

San Giovanni Rotondo is a few miles inland from the Adriatic coast. Originally, it was the site of an ancient pagan temple. The temple had a dome, hence the name "Rotondo." It was a poor and isolated town, and the dwellings were very primitive. There wasn't a plumbing system, electricity, or running water, and there weren't any major roads that went through the hilly town. The Capuchin monastery was connected to the town only by a little trail. It was the kind of place that Padre Pio liked. Upon returning to Foggia, he asked his superiors for permission to join the Capuchin monastery at San Giovanni Rotondo. He was granted permission. Padre Pio returned to San Giovanni Rotondo in September 1916 and mostly remained there for the rest of his life, behind the cloister of the monastery. He never returned to Pietrecina, although God would give him supernatural knowledge now and then of what was going on back in his hometown.

At the end of Padre Pio's reprieve from military service, the police tracked him down at his new residence. They found him at the monastery at San Giovanni Rotondo and arrested him, leading him off to Naples in chains for deserting the military. He explained that he was given a year's reprieve for health reasons and was told to await further orders. He said, "I'm still waiting" (Allegri, 63). They weren't impressed since the authorities in Naples were expecting him to report there to hear his new commands. He was brought before a captain, but the man understood that the whole affair was simply a naïve misunderstanding and cleared him of the charges.

Nonetheless, Padre Pio, known to the State as Francesco Forgione, serial number 2094/25, was required once again to report for military service and admitted for duty. He was assigned to the army barracks at Sales and served there for several months. Later in life, he would often joke about this time in his life, calling it his "100 days in the army," though it was actually longer than that. He had to wear a military uniform, even though it was comically big for him. He wore all the clothes he had at once out of fear that the older soldiers would steal them as a prank. It was a trying chapter in his life, but he especially cherished the time that his father came to visit him and the time he was allowed to return home on a health leave around Christmas. Finally, in March 1918, he was diagnosed with double pneumonia and honorably discharged from the military. At last, he was free to go.

The Stigmata

Back at last at San Giovanni Rotondo, Padre Pio was assigned to oversee a school called the Seraphic College. It provided an education and formation for around 15 boys discerning the religious life. Padre Pio wasn't much of a teacher, but he had a big heart for the boys, and they had great admiration for him. Try as he might, he wasn't very knowledgeable in either grammar or history, the subjects he taught, but the students remembered him for his zeal for holiness and his "humanity." He was also loved as a spiritual director and for his weekly spiritual talks to the boys (*My Life...* ch. 5).

He had already confided to his spiritual director, Padre Benedetto, "I have a vivid desire to offer myself as a victim for perfecting this college that I love tenderly." As if his illnesses had not been enough, Padre Pio would receive more suffering. One day while he was hearing the boys' confessions, Padre Pio had to dismiss the boy in his confessional because of a strange and distressing mystical experience he was having. He writes of that day,

> I was filled with extreme terror at the sight of a heavenly Being who presented himself to the eye of my intellect. In his hand he held some kind of weapon, like a long, sharp-pointed steel blade, which seemed to spew out fire. This Being hurled this weapon into my soul with all his might. It was only with difficulty that I did not cry out. I thought I was dying. I told the boy whose confession I was hearing to leave because I wasn't feeling good and I didn't have

enough strength to continue. This agony lasted uninterruptedly until the morning of August 7. I can't describe how much I suffered during this period of anguish. Even my internal organs were torn and ruptured by that weapon. Since that day I have been mortally wounded. I always feel in the depth of my soul a wound that is always open and that causes me continual agony (Allegri, 72).

This mystical experience is called the "transverberation of the heart" and has been given to numerous saints, including St. Teresa of Avila and St. Philip Neri (*My Life...* Ch. 5). This happened to Padre Pio the day after the Feast of the Transfiguration of Our Lord. Then, on September 20, 1918, on the Friday after the Feast of the Stigmata of St. Francis, Padre Pio received the stigmata in a permanent and visible manner. The stigmata that he had first received in 1910 had become invisible and did not bleed. Thinking at first that he could hide the miraculous wounds, he waited a whole month before writing this in explanation to his spiritual director:

What can I tell you regarding my crucifixion? My God! What embarrassment and humiliation I suffer by being obliged to explain what you have done to this wretched creature!

On the morning of the 20th of last month, in the choir,

after I had celebrated Mass I yielded to a drowsiness similar to a sweet sleep. All the internal and external senses and even the very faculties of my soul were immersed in indescribable stillness. Absolute silence surrounded and invaded me. I was suddenly filled with great peace and abandonment which effaced everything else and caused a lull in the turmoil. All this happened in a flash.

While this was taking place I saw before me a mysterious person similar to the one I had seen on the evening of 5 August. The only difference was that his hands and feet and side were dripping blood. This sight terrified me and what I felt at that moment is indescribable. I thought I should die and really should have died if the Lord had not intervened and strengthened my heart which was about to burst out of my chest.

The vision disappeared and I became aware that my hands, feet and side were dripping blood. (*Letters* Vol. 1, 22 Oct. 1918, quoted in Gallagher, 84)

At times like this, perhaps Padre Pio recalled St. Bonaventure's account of St. Francis receiving the stigmata:

On a certain morning about the Feast of the Exaltation of Holy Cross, while he was praying on the side of the

mountain, he beheld a Seraph having six wings, flaming and resplendent, coming down from the heights of heaven. When in his flight most swift he had reached the space of air nigh the man of God, there appeared betwixt the wings the Figure of a Man crucified, having his hands and feet stretched forth in the shape of a Cross, and fastened unto a Cross. Two wings were raised above His head, twain were spread forth to fly, while twain hid His whole body. Beholding this, Francis was mightily astonished, and joy, mingled with sorrow, filled his heart. He rejoiced at the gracious aspect wherewith he saw Christ, under the guise of the Seraph, regard him, but His crucifixion pierced his soul with a sword of pitying grief....
Accordingly, as the vision disappeared, it left in his heart a wondrous glow, but on his flesh also it imprinted a no less wondrous likeness of its tokens. For forthwith there began to appear in his hands and feet the marks of the nails, even as he had just beheld them in that Figure of the Crucified. For his hands and feet seemed to be pierced through the midst with nails, the heads of the nails shewing in the palms of the hands, and upper side of the feet, and their points shewing on the other side; the heads of the nails were round and black in the hands and feet, while the points were long, bent, and as it were turned back, being formed, of the flesh itself, and protruding

therefrom. The right side, moreover, was—as if it had been pierced by a lance—seamed with a ruddy scar, wherefrom [often] welled the sacred blood, staining his habit and breeches' (8.3).

To some extent, the comparison with the stigmata of St. Francis must have been a comfort, but it was also troubling—not only because it meant physical suffering but also because of the embarrassment that would come from being compared to St. Francis while still living.

St. Francis, the father of Padre Pio's order, was the first known stigmatist. As in the vision of St. Francis, it was the crucified Christ who came to Padre Pio, offering and inflicting the wounds. St. Francis had difficulty walking because of the stigmata on his feet. Likewise Padre Pio, after receiving the stigmata, hobbled back to his room, hardly able to walk because of the pain in his feet. St. Francis' experience of the stigmata, with its continual bleeding from the hands, feet, and side soaking into any fabric, was similar to that of Padre Pio. Once he got back to his room, Padre Pio tried to control the bleeding, but the bleeding never stopped. Nor did the wound ever become infected. He found a cloth to drape over his hands to hide the wounds, but in the course of daily life and ministry, it was clear that there was something very unusual. St. Francis also tried to hide his wounds as much as possible. In particular, hardly anyone was given to see the wound in his side. Once when a brother was massaging the infirm St. Francis' back, he reached for the wound in his side. Immediately the saint cried out in pain (St. Bonaventure 8.8).

Despite his spiritual experiences, and perhaps even because of them, Padre Pio felt far from God. He even said, "Who knows if God is happy with me" (*My Life...*ch. 5). He was entering into the "dark night of the soul," a period of crisis in which the consolation of God's presence seems far away. On the path of spiritual perfection, such periods have been recognized by the saints as necessary for birthing new levels of closeness with God.

Life with the Stigmata

A woman at Mass was the first to notice Padre Pio's stigmata. Vittoria Ventrella recalls, "My sister Filomena went to the convent on September 20, 1918, and was the first to notice that the Padre had received the wounds, because she saw on his hands the red marks similar to the marks that we see on the statue of the Sacred Heart. She came home and told us" (*My Life...* ch. 5). The next day, another lady noticed the wounds and went to one of the friars, Padre Paolino da Casacalenda, and told him about it. Padre Paolino recalled, "I started thinking: 'How can [it] be possible that Padre Pio has received the stigmata without me realizing it? I am always with him.' I went in Padre Pio's room without knocking at the door. He was writing at the desk. When he saw me he got up. I asked him to continue writing. I got closer, and first saw the wound on the back and on the palm of the right hand. Then I saw the one on the back of the left hand." Padre Paolino then wrote to Padre Benedetto, the superior, about the matter; the superior simply commanded him to silence. Padre Benedetto did not even notify the head of the order for some time, hoping to prevent a stir. At first, he did not even want to go to see for himself.

Whatever the motives for silence, they were not unfounded since the supernatural wounds became a cause of trouble for both Padre Pio and the order. Silence from the order, however, did little to help the situation since all the people of San Giovanni Rotondo and the surrounding area came to know about the friar's stigmata from the talk that went around. People from all over the region began flocking to the monastery to see the living saint. As a result, Padre Pio became subject to endless medical examinations to determine the origin of the wounds, the best care for them, and whether there was any danger to others. Since he had been previously diagnosed with tuberculosis, some other friars worried that they might contract the disease from contact with blood from his wounds. His superiors, meanwhile, wanted to know the exact origin of the wounds.

For us, the many medical examinations of the wounds by medical professionals, both believers and atheists, leave us with scientific documentation and observation of what took place in Padre Pio's body. The reports tell us that the wounds were round, about the size of a penny. Some said light could be seen coming through the wounds, if there was a light source on the other side. Many doctors made attempts to stop the bleeding, but there was no use. They bled constantly though they would scab over to some extent. X-Rays showed that there was no damage to the bone or cartilage, and observations revealed that there was no damage to any of the surrounding tissue, as would happen from a puncture wound or from an acid burn. There was also no infection, as would come from a lesion induced by disease. Doctors also noted Padre Pio's demeanor, which they tended to agree was sincere and not apt to create a farce. Many of the doctors concluded that the wounds were beyond what medical science was able to account for. Even an atheist doctor concluded that they were at least certainly not forgeries (*My Life...* ch. 6).

Dr. Festa, a medical doctor who examined Padre Pio in the early days of his stigmata, wrote the following about the wounds in his feet:

> During my examination, in order to be able to study also the lesions of his feet, I myself helped him remove his stockings, which I immediately observed were abundantly stained with bloody serum. On top of both feet, and precisely corresponding with the second metatarsus (part of the foot between the tarsus and the toes), I found here also a circular lesion, of reddish brown color covered with a soft scab, which duplicated exactly the origin and characteristics of those described in the hands; perhaps these were a little smaller and more superficial. There is perfect completeness of the metatarsus bone lying under with full length; there is no trace of infiltration, no swelling, no inflammatory reaction in the skin which surrounds it; also here there is light but continuous drops of bloody serum.
>
> On the bottom of the feet and at a point corresponding to the top of the feet, there appeared at my observations two other lesions; one in each sole of the foot, well outlined in

their edges, perfectly identical to the top wounds, and bleeding.

Direct pressing of any of the wounds causes very intense pain and the mere touching of the tissues that surround the wounds gives pain, but less pain. He has pain in both feet and this causes him to walk slowly with an uncertain gait. The author noticed that when Pio descended the altar steps to give Holy Communion, he had to turn around and step down backwards. There is less pain in the feet by stepping down backwards. (Carty, 286)

Dr. Begnami, an atheist who would not consider the possibility of the supernatural, was nonetheless convinced that Padre Pio was not intentionally faking the stigmata and that its features were beyond the ability of science to understand. He writes, "I definitely can't support [that they might have been artificially and voluntarily produced], especially lacking a direct proof.... The impression of sincerity that Padre Pio gives me, keeps me definitively from thinking of simulation.... What cannot be explained by what we know about the neurotic necrosis is the perfectly symmetrical localization of the described lesions, and their persistence without noticeable changes, as the patient states" (*My Life...* ch. 6).

Padre Benedetto, then the Capuchin provincial superior , and finally the Vatican offices under Pope Benedict XV also got involved with the examination process. The Pope sent a number of high-ranking Church officials to examine Padre Pio from a spiritual and holistic perspective, and several were thoroughly convinced of the supernatural origin of the wounds and the holiness of Padre Pio's life. Archbishop Kenealy, who was particularly known for his skepticism surrounding supernatural phenomena, wrote this: "I wanted to see the wounds of Padre Pio because I am resistant to believe in things if I have not seen them with my own eyes. I went, I saw, I was conquered (*Veni, Vidi, Victus sum*). I am deeply convinced that we have a true saint here. The Lord, with the five wounds of the Passion has given him great gifts, and he is completely at ease. If he knows how to suffer, he also knows how to laugh" (*My Life...* ch. 6).

A man named Carlo Campanini mentioned to his doctor his intention to visit Padre Pio. A source tells us, "The doctor replied: 'He is a hysterical who got the wound by thinking too much about Jesus on the Cross.' When Campanini visited Padre Pio, he told him: 'When you see your doctor, tell him to think intensely about being an ox. Let's see if he grows horns'" (*My Life...* ch. 23).

Persecution

One priest, however, sent back a negative report to the Holy Office, the Vatican office at the time responsible for preserving the integrity of the Faith and investigating alleged supernatural occurrences. His name was Padre Agostino Gemelli, a Franciscan priest, psychologist, and consultant to the Holy Office. He was never actually able to examine the wounds or to administer a formal exam of any type. While Padre Pio was busy preparing for Mass, Padre Gemelli approached him with his intention to examine his wounds. Padre Pio requested to see a note of authorization, which he did not have. So Padre Pio declined to be examined by him. Instead, Padre Gemelli based his report to the Holy Office on what he called "precious psychological data through a shrewd questioning" (*My Life...* ch. 6). He claimed that Padre Pio was a man of little intelligence and shallow spirituality who certainly could not be the subject of such a supernatural wonder. Dr. Festa objected to Padre Gemelli's unscientific methodology, but the Holy Office took notice and decided to intervene. Padre Gemelli was later confronted about how he could be so confident in his claims about Padre Pio without having actually examined him, but he gave only an angry retort.

The Holy Office had also heard a number of outlandish false charges from secular clergy regarding Padre Pio's personal conduct. Some of Padre Pio's enemies even crafted detailed "witness" accounts of Padre Pio's alleged sexual misconduct with women, and they accused him of being possessed by the devil and of putting on makeup as part of a satanic practice. They also accused his Capuchin superiors of capitalizing on Padre Pio's notoriety for monetary gain and of living a life of luxury. The local clergy were most likely jealous because worshippers left the parish churches for Mass at the Capuchin monastery. Pasquale Gagliardi, archbishop of Manfredonia, which included San Giovanni Rotundo, led the charge against Padre Pio with these false reports to the Vatican. The local priest, Don Palladino, reported that he regretted the day he gave Padre Pio permission to hear Confessions, since he leaves penitents "in a state of agitation" (Ruffin, 189).

Furthermore, it was made known to the Holy Office that Padre Pio had access to carbolic acid since he was assigned to the care of sick novices during a Spanish fever epidemic. Some suspected that he used the acid to create his wounds. The Vatican was not skeptical about the possibility of phenomena such as the stigmata, but it was quite skeptical that Padre Pio, in particular, could be a legitimate recipient of these sacred wounds.

In 1923, Cardinal Merry del Val of the Holy Office gave Padre Pio a disposition order forbidding him from blessing the faithful from his window, from showing the "so-called stigmata," from creating any disturbance, and even from communicating with his provincial superior and spiritual director Padre Benedetto, whom the Holy Office suspected of giving poor direction. The disposition also warned the faithful not to regard phenomena surrounding Padre Pio as being of divine origin.

The disposition order was published in the Vatican newspaper, *L'Osservatore Romano*, and also in the Capuchin periodical. The friars hid the Vatican newspaper from Padre Pio, but later he came upon the Capuchin periodical at the dinner table. They tried to prevent him from reading it, but he opened up to the exact page where the disposition was published. He showed no emotion and even expressed his willingness to follow any orders to have him transferred out of San Giovanni Rotondo. But Padre Pio could not completely extinguish the pain he felt. Allegri recounts, "When recreation was over, his superior walked with him to his cell. Padre Pio went straight to the window of his room to close the blinds, but remained there without moving, looking at the plains below. Then he turned around abruptly and broke down in tears" (98).

The Vatican's order was intended to dissuade people from visiting Padre Pio, but it did not succeed in doing that. Cardinal Merry Del Val recommended in the disposition that Padre Pio be transferred once the conditions were right. This, however, was not possible and would never come about. The people of San Giovanni Rotondo were accustomed to violence, and now that they had a saint in their poor town, they were ready to resort to violence once again to keep him there. Already in 1919 and again in 1920, the local people rose up in response to rumors of a possible transfer of their saint.

Already in 1923, when Padre Pio didn't show up for Mass because he was ordered by his Capuchin superiors to say it only in private, the mayor of San Giovanni Rotondo formed the "People's Association" to intervene. In this incident, 5,000 townspeople besieged the monastery and constructed a barricade, and armed guards were stationed to keep watch. The mayor, Don Morcaldi, told Padre Ignazio, the guardian of the monastery who had received the order from higher up, "I will resign as mayor and fight as an ordinary citizen in the riot that will ensue!" (Ruffin, 194). Rioters even attacked the house of the Don Palladino, the parish priest in town who used to preach against Padre Pio and tell false stories about him. Overwhelmed by all of this, Padre Ignazio felt compelled to give into the people's demands.

With word of another attempt to transfer Padre Pio, the people threatened violence and bloodshed. Archbishop Gagliardi, who was party to the false reports against Padre Pio to the Vatican, went out to the people with a faked smile, insisting that he would protect Padre Pio and keep him with them forever. It became clear that the only way to transfer Padre Pio was over the dead bodies of those who would likely be killed in the rioting. Mayor Morcaldi used no uncertain terms when speaking with a cardinal from the Vatican: "If Padre Pio had to leave San

Giovanni Rotondo for a just reason, we would accompany him from town with music and banners. But if he must leave as one guilty of a crime, at the instigation of an immoral, belligerent, and dishonest clergy who would continue to corrupt our population after banishing a holy priest with ignominy, then Your Eminence, I will throw away [the insignia of my office] and, in order to take Padre Pio away, you will have to trample on our dead bodies!" (Ruffin, 195).

Not long after the disposition from the Holy Office, Padre Guisseppantonio, the Capuchin minister general, again forbade Padre Pio from saying Mass in public. After that, Padre Pio had to alternate the times of his Masses, which were said in a private chapel, so that the people would not know when they would be. The people found out nonetheless, even though they were not allowed into the Mass. Furthermore, the Holy Office intervened once again, forbidding Padre Pio from even writing to anyone by letter. Many people wrote to him each day to ask for prayers and seek his advice—even a king wrote to him—but Padre Pio could not reply; he could only pray for them. Padre Pio had taken into his care the souls of many people, whom he called his "spiritual children," and he had written them many beautiful and deep letters to help them in their spiritual lives. These letters, too, had to stop (Allegri, 102–103).

Confined and Set Free

Padre Pio was truly a man of suffering. Renzo Allegri writes,

> During his entire life, he was defamed by vulgar
> accusations and accused of being a vile swindler. He was
> punished and imprisoned. He died without having ever
> been officially rehabilitated. When he died, his name was
> still on the list of people condemned by the Holy Office.
> Any attempt to deny these facts would amount to
> censorship, and would do Padre Pio one more wrong. His
> love, his goodness, this heroic virtue, and above all his
> holiness stand out precisely because he never complained
> and never criticized anyone even though he was
> persecuted by his "family"—some representatives of the
> Church and some of his fellow monks. (93)

A number of supporters of Padre Pio took matters into their own
hands to try to help him. The People's Association sent out
telegrams to authorities all over Italy, telling them of Padre Pio's
righteousness and their desire to keep him. Others brought
evidence to light that uncovered the real motives of Padre Pio's
detractors and proved that the accusations leveled against him
were false. One of them, by the name of Emmanuel Brunnato,
even hired a spy to find out the truth about Padre Pio's
detractors and wrote a book with his shocking findings of
clerical corruption. The Holy Office, however, placed the book on
the Index of Forbidden Books and collected all known copies.

Padre Pio's supporters then went to the Vatican to show them the evidence of the corruption that lay behind the war against Padre Pio and testimony about the friar's holiness of life. The irrefutable evidence of corruption and misdoings led to the removal of Don Palladino's priestly faculties in 1927, though Gagliardi, the corrupt archbishop of Manfredonia, was able to get his friend out of trouble by allowing him to say Mass and to live in his luxurious house before being reassigned as pastor of another parish in Manfredonia. The archbishop's friends at the Vatican did not want to do anything to Gagliardi, even after a great many priests from his archdiocese signed a letter to the Vatican attesting to the truth of the charges against him. Instead, they required all the signers of the letter to undergo penitential exercises at a retreat in Naples. With more pressure from Padre Pio's supporters and with the threat of another book coming out against the Vatican, Archbishop Gagliardi was finally removed from office in 1929.

Despite his main detractors being unmasked, the situation did not improve for Padre Pio. Instead, the Holy Office reaffirmed its condemnation of him, suspended him from all priestly duties except saying Mass in private, and forbade him from communicating with the outside or even so much as looking out the window of his monastery. This was what Padre Pio called his two years of imprisonment. He spent this time praying for his spiritual children, reading spiritual books, meditating on Christ's passion, and occasionally crafting some bad puns to share with the friars. While this time was difficult for Padre Pio, he relished in the sweetness of prayer; nothing, to him, was sweeter than his time with God, in which he would hear God speaking to him and converse with angels and saints.

Meanwhile, Don Morcaldi wrote another book in defense of Padre Pio that unveiled the corruption in the local church. Cardinal Rossi at the Vatican pleaded with Morcadli to stop, so Morcaldi made a deal with him to deliver the books up to the cardinal on the condition that Padre Pio would be freed from his imprisonment. The Vatican, however, did not hold up their side of the bargain. So then Brunnato, after a few more unsuccessful discussions with the Vatican, published another book on the subject, this time outside of Italy. The readers were outraged and flooded the Vatican with letters protesting the injustices. The letters from the outside world, a book by Dr. Festa on the inability of science to explain Padre Pio's stigmata, and a report from religious close to Padre Pio about his holiness of life finally made it to the ear of Pope Pius XI, who ultimately gave Padre Pio his freedom in 1933.

The Meaning of the Stigmata

Redemptive suffering, however, was in the very meaning of the sacred stigmata. Saints throughout the ages have found that the deeper they go into the spiritual life, the more suffering seems to come their way.

According to Christian belief, the division between God and humanity came as a result of a decision on the part of our first parents, Adam and Eve, to turn away from God. This resulted in a withdrawal of God's grace, a general tendency to sin, and the punishment of suffering, death, and damnation. The ultimate remedy for this situation came in Jesus Christ, who alone was able to atone fully for the sins of humanity since he was fully God and fully human.

But there is more. St. Paul writes in his Letter to the Colossians, "Now I rejoice in my sufferings for your sake, and in my flesh I am filling up what is lacking in the afflictions of Christ on behalf of his body, which is the church" (Col. 1:24). Objectively speaking, nothing could possibly be lacking in the sufferings of Jesus. Not only did he endure horrendous suffering out of obedience to the Father, but also the love he offered was infinite since he was God made man. What is lacking is the participation of the members of his body in the Church. God allows for the suffering of his people to become joined to the suffering of Christ; he makes those sufferings have redemptive value. According to the *Catechism of the Catholic Church,* for those who are in Christ and offer up their sufferings, "Suffering, a consequence of original sin, acquires a new meaning; it becomes a participation in the saving work of Jesus" (no. 1521).

St. Paul further writes in his Letter to the Galatians, "I have been crucified with Christ; yet I live, no longer I, but Christ lives in me; insofar as I now live in the flesh, I live by faith in the Son of God who has loved me and given himself up for me" (Gal. 2:19–20). Here he talks of a death to the old self through a participation in Christ's suffering and death and a rising of the new self in Christ. This is true for all true Christians. He writes in his Letter to the Romans, "Are you unaware that we who were baptized into Christ Jesus were baptized into his death?" (Rom. 6:3). Because of the human condition and God's plan for its healing, suffering in fact has an essential place in the Christian life. St. Paul writes further, "The Spirit itself bears witness with our spirit that we are children of God, and if children, then heirs, heirs of God and joint heirs with Christ, if only we suffer with him so that we may also be glorified with him" (Rom. 8:16–17).

The *Catechism* explains that the free gift of being made children of God also gives our suffering redemptive value. We read in the *Catechism*, "The merit of man before God in the Christian life arises from the fact that God *has freely chosen to associate man with the work of his grace.* The fatherly action of God is first on his own initiative, and then follows man's free acting through his collaboration, so that the merit of good works is to be attributed in the first place to the grace of God, then to the faithful. Man's merit, moreover, itself is due to God, for his good actions proceed in Christ, from the predispositions and assistance given by the Hoy Spirit" (no. 2008). Further, the *Catechism* explains that our suffering can even have redemptive value for others: "Moved by the Holy Spirit and by charity, *we can then merit* for ourselves and for others the graces needed for our sanctification, for the increase of grace and charity, and for the attainment of eternal life. Even temporal goods like health and friendship can be merited in accordance with God's wisdom" (no. 2010). This would, of course, not be possible without Christ's suffering since the stigmata are but a participation in it. Further, the *Catechism* explains that the grace of justification can be won solely by Christ's passion but that the merits of the saints can contribute to the distribution of actual graces.

While the first recorded instance of the stigmata was with St. Francis of Assisi in the thirteenth century, St. Paul speaks in a mysterious way in his Letter to the Galatians of his own sufferings in relation to Christ's wounds. He writes, "From now on, let no one make troubles for me; for I bear the marks of Jesus on my body" (Gal. 6:17).

The stigmata, which since the time of St. Francis have appeared in the bodies of several hundred saintly individuals, are a symbol of participation in Christ's suffering and are always accompanied by physical pain, emotional suffering, and mystical experiences. A theologian writes,

The sufferings may be considered the essential part of visible stigmata; the substance of this grace consists of pity for Christ, participation in His sufferings, sorrows, and for the same end—the expiation of the sins unceasingly committed in the world. If the sufferings were absent, the wounds would be but an empty symbol, theatrical representation, conducing to pride. If the stigmata really come from God, it would be unworthy of His wisdom to participate in such futility, and to do so by a miracle.

But this trial is far from being the only one which the saints have to endure: "The life of stigmatics," says Dr. Imbert, "is but a long series of sorrows which arise from the Divine malady of the stigmata and end only in death. It seems historically certain that ecstatics [people who experience ecstasies] alone bear the stigmata; moreover, they have visions which correspond to their rôle of co-sufferers, beholding from time to time the blood-stained scenes of the Passion (Augustin Poulin, "Mystical Stigmata," New Advent Encyclopedia).

Thus, Padre Pio's sufferings were given to him for redemptive value, and his experience was common to other stigmatics throughout history. He understood that he was specially chosen to suffer for the spiritual good of others. In fact, he once said, "I started suffering since I was in my mother's womb" (*My Life...* ch.

27). He offered himself to God as a victim on several occasions. In one letter to Padre Benedetto, he wrote, "On other occasions I offered myself to the Lord as a victim for poor sinners and souls in Purgatory. This has grown continuously in my heart, and now it has become a powerful passion."

St. Bonaventure likewise related numerous stories of how the wounds of St. Francis' stigmata brought help and healing to others. He wrote of how the water used to cleanse his wounds was able to bring restoration to farmers' livestock that were dying from plague and risking the health of the community: "Wondrous to relate, so soon as the sprinkling, were it but a drop, fell upon the sick animals as they lay on the ground, they recovered their former strength, and got up forthwith, and, as though they had felt no sickness, hastened unto the pastures! Thus it befell, through the marvellous virtue of that water that had touched the sacred wounds, that the whole plague was at once stayed, and the contagious sickness banished from the flocks and herds" (8.6).

Padre Pio's mother, Mamma Peppa, however, did not at first understand the meaning of her son's wounds. Instead, hearing reports that he was "wounded," she began to spend a great deal of time in San Giovanni Rotondo starting in 1919 out of great concern for his health (Allegri, 108). She attended her son's Masses every day and eventually understood the meaning of the stigmata. She died at San Giovanni Rotondo in 1929 with her son at her side, and Orazio died there in 1944, also with his son kneeling by his bed.

Bilocation

God gave Padre Pio spiritual gifts to help him in his difficulties and in the difficulties of those for whom he interceded and counseled.

The Holy Office's disposition against Padre Pio and Padre Benedetto communicating with each other was particularly difficult for the two men. Padre Benedetto, though he had often given Padre Pio strict orders with the intention of enforcing the rule of living within community, had become a true spiritual father to Padre Pio. The parting lasted until Padre Benedetto's death some 20 years later. Padre Benedetto was asked on his deathbed if Padre Pio should be sent for to say a final goodbye. He replied, "No, it is not necessary. He is here beside me" (Ruffin, 192). This was likely one of the many reported incidents in which Padre Pio was said to 'bilocate.' Sometimes when Padre Pio would pray, he would be physically present both in his place of prayer and also with the person he was praying for, since his body was so thoroughly subjected to his spirit. The first time this happened to him was at the age of 17.

It seems that St. Francis, too, was given the gift of bilocation. St. Bonaventure wrote, "In what wise Francis showed himself present unto them that were absent, by the working of the divine power, is clearly apparent from what hath been afore related, if we recall unto mind how in his absence he appeared unto the Brethren as one transfigured, in a chariot of fire, and how at the Chapter of Arles he shewed himself with arms outstretched after the likeness of a Cross. This we must believe to have been wrought by the divine ruling, that by the miraculous appearance of his bodily presence it might be abundantly evident how that his spirit was present in and penetrated by the light of the eternal wisdom, which is more moving than any motion, and goeth through all things by reason of her pureness, and entering into holy souls maketh them friends of God, and prophets" (11.14).

Pope Pius XI did not have the time to look into Padre Pio's situation personally because of the tense global situation at the time. Instead, he had to rely on the reports that were given to him. Believing that Padre Pio had instigated the rioters to protect himself against the orders of his superiors, the Holy Father was considering having Padre Pio barred from exercising his priestly faculties. Just then, according to a story retold by one of the cardinals present, Padre Pio bilocated before the Pope, kissed his ring, sought his blessing, and asked him not to do what he had planned. After that time, the Church relented in its harder demands against Padre Pio (Ruffin, 198).

From the early days of his priesthood, Padre Pio accepted into the care "spiritual children"— individuals for whom he would pray, offer his sufferings, and provide spiritual direction. He committed himself to ensuring their salvation and spiritual growth. At first, several women in town asked to become his spiritual children, but then the circle grew to include people far and wide. Still, he would not accept just anyone as a spiritual child; he had to know the person well enough to ensure that he or she was serious about the spiritual life. After his "imprisonment" was over and he was no longer forbidden to communicate, Padre Pio used his powers of bilocation to be with his spiritual children in a way never possible merely by letter.

There are many stories of his bilocation, especially from his spiritual children. In 1954, Padre Carmelo Durante, Padre Pio's superior at the time, gathered some of Padre Pio's early spiritual children for several meetings to find out more about his early days in San Giovanni Rotondo. One of his spiritual children, Rosinella Gisolfi, told him that she saw Padre Pio present at the meetings. She was one of Padre Pio's first spiritual children, and she had witnessed his bilocation since his early days in town. Padre Carmelo asked the other friars what Padre Pio was doing that evening. They replied, "The usual: he conducted the evening Benediction, then he received his friends and we chatted together."

So then Padre Carmelo gathered his courage to ask Padre Pio himself, who had greeting him after coming back from the meeting. He recalls, "That evening I replied at once, also so as to get the conversation going: 'Yes Father, I have returned; everything went well. Your spiritual children are very happy. But I would like to ask you one thing!' And he: 'Yes, what is it?' I began: 'Padre, Rosinella...' and then I lost courage. And he, with a strategy all his own (who could ever understand the Padre!): 'Rosinella? Is she not well?' If anyone I was the one who felt not well now! 'No, Padre, she is well.' 'And so?' he went on. I took the plunge: 'Padre, Rosinella said that you are always present at our meetings!' And quite untroubled he answered: 'Well? Don't you want me? Don't you want me to come to these meetings?'" (*Voice of Padre Pio,* Nov. 1998 quoted on ewtn.com/padrepio).

Padre Carmelo also recalls how Padre Pio would bring edification to his spiritual children through his bilocation:

> In one meeting an unusual thing happened. At a certain point a few members of the group began to speak badly about some people. It got a little out of hand when suddenly Rosinella frightened exclaimed: "Father Guardian, Padre Pio has an angry face!" We were all scared and quickly stopped and not without some embarrassment and self accusation began to speak well of these people. A few minutes later I asked Rosinella: "Now how does Padre Pio look?" And she: "He looks calm!" We were happy again, and had learnt our lesson to not speak badly of people.

Here is another fascinating story about Padre Pio's bilocations from Padre Carmello:

> One day in the refectory we were talking of this and that.

I remember that in the conversation I was holding forth about a fact then unheard of: an aeroplane—I don't remember of which airline—had made the journey non-stop between Rome and New York in only six hours. To me and the others it seemed something incredible!

The Padre who until then had kept silent, interrupted in the middle and asked: "How long? How many hours, did you say?"

I answered, with increasing marvel: "Padre, six hours and what is more non-stop!"

The Padre also marveled over the fact but to the side exclaimed: "Six hours! Good heavens, but that is a long time! When I go it takes me only a second."

We asked him to explain himself, but he would say no more and only repeated: "I told you! I told you!"

Ruffin cites this story retold by an American priest: "A lady in Chicago had written several times asking [prayer] for her sick son who was married and had two children. In her last letter she wrote that her son had died a peaceful death. The Drs. had feared a violent struggle. Five days before the young man's death the mother visited him in the hospital. He told her: 'This morning Fr. Pio stood right there,' pointing to where the mother stood" (326).

Ruffin also recounts this story: "Once Padre Eusebio Notte, speaking of a mutual acquaintance, asked, 'Padre Pio, you know that man's house in Rome, don't you?' Pio responded: 'Me? How could I know it when I haven't been away from the friary for ever so many years?' When Eusebio persisted, 'But, Padre, this man says you went to his house and that he saw you,' Pio responded, 'Ah, but that's a different matter. When these things occur ... the Lord only permits the person concerned to be seen, not the surroundings'" (329).

What exactly is bilocation? Padre Pio tells us that it is an "extension of body and soul." Ruffin writes, "Once, when someone asked cautiously if those who experience the phenomenon of bilocation know where they are going and what they are doing, Pio, replied, 'Certainly they know. Perhaps they don't know whether it is the body or the soul that goes, but they are fully conscious of what is happening, and they know where they are going'" (329).

Padre Pio was also known to have the related gift of levitation—being suspended in air. According to Fr. Carty, this happened to Padre Pio during World War II and was witnessed by American fighter pilots. He writes,

> [Padre Pio] assured the people of San Giovanni that their town would not be bombed. During the war the Americans had an air base at Bari, about 75 miles from

San Giovanni. There were still Germans in the neighborhood and the American officer in charge at Bari heard that they had a munitions dump in or near San Giovanni Rotondo. So he called his officers, planned a raid and said he would lead in the first plane. He was a Protestant. When they neared San Giovanni Rotondo, he saw high in the air, ahead of his plane, a monk with arms outstretched as if to ward off his coming. The General was stupefied. He ordered the formation to return to base and drop the bombs in an open field where they would do no harm to their landing planes. When he returned to the base and was asked how things had gone, he related what he had seen. An Italian officer told him there was a monk at San Giovanni Rotondo, whom the people consider a saint. Probably he was the one the officer saw in the heavens. The officer determined to find out. He and another officer went to San Giovanni and together they went to the sacristy with other layman to watch as the fathers came down for Mass. He immediately recognized Padre Pio as the one he had seen high in the air in front of his plane. (23–24)

Confessor and Celebrant

Each day, Padre Pio spent 15 to 19 hours in the confessional as people flooded the monastery at San Giovanni Rotondo to confess to this holy priest. He hardly even stopped to eat. Having the gift of reading hearts, Padre Pio would often be given to know things about the penitents that would not naturally be possible for him to know. This is not to say that he was all-knowing but that he was given to know supernaturally certain matters that pertained to his ministry.

A man named Friedrich Abresch from Germany had heard remarkable things about Padre Pio and decided to make the trip to see for himself. He had converted to Catholicism to marry his wife but did not really practice the faith. He approached Padre Pio for Confession, but the sacrament, to him, was merely a psychological exercise, and his beliefs and practices were not consistent with the faith. He did not reveal these points to Padre Pio, but the friar perceived this supernaturally and pointed it out to him. Padre Pio aimed at bringing about an inner conversion in the man and thus sent him away for reflection before giving him absolution. The man was amazed by Padre Pio's knowledge of his life and realized that all he said was true. But he had a hard time finishing the task the holy man had given him of examining his conscience for the sins he had committed since his last "good Confession." He could not even think of when that was. When he returned to Padre Pio's confessional, the priest reminded him:

"Yes, you made a good confession that time when you were returning from your wedding trip, let us leave out all the rest, and begin from there." I was struck with the overwhelming realization that I had come in contact with the supernatural. But the Father did not give me time to think, concealing his knowledge of my entire past under the form of questions. He enumerated with precision and clarity all of my faults, even mentioning the number of times that I had missed Mass. After the Father has specified all of my mortal sins, he made me understand, with most impressive words the whole of their gravity, adding in a tone of voice that I can never forget: "You have launched a hymn to Satan, whereas Jesus in his tremendous love has broken his neck for you." He then gave me a penance and absolved me. This absolution gave me a feeling of suffocation at the time, but later caused me such joy and such a sensation of lightness. Returning to the village with the other pilgrims, I behaved like a noisy child.

...I was from the first completely bowled over by hearing of things that I had quite forgotten, and I was only able to reconstruct the past by remembering in all their detail the particulars that Padre Pio had described with such precision." (Carty, 107–109)

Though not a priest able to hear confessions, St. Francis too was given supernatural knowledge of situations that were brought to his attention. St. Bonaventure wrote of him, "Once two Brethren were come from Terra di Lavoro, the elder of whom had given some offense unto the younger. But when they came before the Father, he asked of the younger how the Brother that was his companion had behaved toward him on the way. On his making answer: 'Well enough,' he responded: 'Beware, Brother, that thou lie not under pretext of humility, for I know, I know,— do thou wait a while and thou shalt see.' The Brother was mightily astonished in what wise he had perceived in spirit what had taken place so far off" (11.13).

Padre Pio was not an easy confessor. He was known to be severe with penitents and sometimes to send them away until they were truly sorry for their sins and ready to amend their lives. According to one source, "A certain man had the reputation of being a good Catholic, admired and esteemed by all who knew him. Actually he was living in sin. He had neglected his wife, and was now compensating for his loneliness by a relationship with another woman. On one occasion he went to confession to Padre Pio. In order to justify himself, he started talking about a 'spiritual crisis.' But he had not counted on facing an 'extraordinary' confessor. Padre Pio stood up at once and shouted, 'What spiritual crisis? You are a litterbug! And God is angry with you. Go away!'" (padrepio.catholicwebservices.com).

The same source reports on how Padre Pio dealt with two penitents who swore against the Blessed Virgin Mary while having car trouble: "...the driver lost his calm and full of anger he cursed. The day after the two men went to St. Giovanni Rotondo where one of the men had a sister. With the help of his sister they succeeded in going to Padre Pio to confession. The first man entered the confessional but Padre Pio sent him away. Then it was the turn of the driver. He started saying something to Padre Pio: 'I have been angry.' But Padre Pio shouted: 'Wretch! You have cursed our Mother! What did she do to you, Our Lady?' Then he sent him away as well."

Many callous souls were softened in Padre Pio's confessional, including Masons, prominent Communists, actors and actresses swept up in the glamor of the world, men having adulterous affairs, and secularized people who had little use for religion. Not all of Padre Pio's supernatural knowledge was directed at softening the hearts of sinners, however; he was also known to have arranged numerous happy Catholic marriages through his special knowledge of God's plan.

His Masses also moved the hearts of many. Padre Pio took a very long time to say Mass because he would be communicating with God and heavenly beings during the holy sacrifice and because he felt Christ's sacrifice within himself. People who attended his Masses said it was very touching to see how he prayed the Mass. Ruffin recounts the experience of American serviceman Bill

Carrigan, who attended his Masses while the U. S. troops were in Italy during World War II: "Carrigan noticed a transformation in the celebrant during the consecration. He seemed to take on physical sufferings. Although he knew nothing at the time of Padre Pio's stigmata, Carrigan noticed that the Capuchin leaned on the altar, first on one elbow and then on the other, as if he were trying to relieve the pain in his speaking the words, '*Hoc est enim corpus meum.*' ('This is my body.') 'as if he were in physical pain.' When he reached for the chalice, he jerked his hand back violently, 'as if the pain were so great he could not grasp it.' His facial muscles were twitching and tears were rolling down his cheeks. Occasionally, he jerked his head to one side or the other, as if he were suffering blows to the head and neck" (258). Carrigan later went on to promote interest in Padre Pio in the U.S. after the war.

Elsewhere Ruffin writes of Padre Pio's supernatural Masses,

> ...many people who knew Padre Pio insist that the most impressive feature of his ministry was his Mass, which, according to one Italian journal, made worshipers feel as if they were at the foot of the cross. A Salesian priest observed that when Padre Pio celebrated, "the most intimate fibers of my being vibrated with feelings of emotion and sweetness which I had never before experienced." Another witness said that it seemed as if Padre Pio, in saying Mass, "came from another humanity

superior to ours, speaking ... through an atmosphere beyond this life." Padre Gerardo Di Flumeri described Padre Pio's Mass as "a supernatural Mass."

What made the Mass supernatural? Padre Pio, who defined the Mass as "a sacred fix with the Passion of Jesus," in which "all Calvary" was presented again, extended into the present, admitted to an intense mystical involvement with the unseen world. Apart from any merit or worthiness on his part, he was allowed to relive Jesus' Passion in a direct way. "All that Jesus has suffered in His Passion, inadequately I also suffer, as far as is possible for a human being. And all this against my unworthiness, and thanks only to His goodness." (291–292)

Padre Pio, in fact, was simply able to experience what the Church believes to take place in every Mass. According to the *Catechism of the Catholic Church*, "The Eucharist is thus a sacrifice because it *re-presents* (makes present) the sacrifice of the cross" (no. 1366).

Miracles and Healings

Like St. Francis, the founder of his order, Padre Pio was known to have worked many miracles and healings. In fact, Padre Pio was not finished intervening in the life of Friedrich Abresch, the non-practicing Catholic mentioned above who had come to his confessional from Germany. Ruffin writes,

> In 1926, a year later, Abresch's wife began to hemorrhage, and the doctors diagnosed a tumor in her womb. After two years, the tumor had grown alarmingly. Several doctors advised her to submit to surgery without delay. But she was devastated by the certainty that a hysterectomy would leave her incapable of bearing children, so she went to Padre Pio. At first he advised her to have the operation, but when she told him of her desperate desire to have at least one child, he changed his mind and told her not to submit to the knife. After that the hemorrhages ceased and, although the tumor remained, to her great delight, she conceived and, at the age of nearly 40, gave birth to a son. The boy, who was named Pio, later became a monsignor.

> Eventually the Abresch family settled in San Giovanni Rotondo, where Freidrich opened a photography studio. For many years he was something of an official photographer for Padre Pio and his brethren, and most of the extent likenesses of the celebrated priest were taken by this man, who was led to Christ through his ministry. (207)

Even from early on in his ministry, Padre Pio's miracles became widely known. Allegri writes,

> The first newspaper article about Padre Pio, which was published in Naples *Mattino* on June 21, 1919, mentioned his miracles. In headline was spread across six columns: *Padre Pio, The Saint of San Giovanni Rotondo, Works a Miracle for the Region's Chancellor.* It described the experience of Pasquale Di Chiara, thirty-six, who was chancellor of the Prefecture of San Giovanni Rotondo. He had been forced to use a cane in order to walk after suffering a fall several months earlier. Padre Pio commanded him to walk when he saw him. Di Chiara described his experience to the journalists: "I felt a strong burning sensation in my foot, that soon spread throughout my body. I began to walk perfectly without any need for assistance."
>
> The newspaper also referred to the fact that Pasquale Di Chiara's daughter had also experienced a miraculous healing. The victim of infantile paralysis, she had been using braces on her legs. But when Padre Pio told her to take them off, she was able to walk and never used them again.

A great many people came to Padre Pio with their ailments and experienced inexplicable recoveries. Sometimes Padre Pio would bilocate to bring peace and healing to the infirm person far away.

Often, with Padre Pio's presence, people would sense what is called the 'odor of sanctity.' Some compared it to the smell of lilies, violets, and roses, but it was sensed in places where none of these things were. Fr. Charles Carty writes,

> The phenomenon of perfume, a singular gift of the servant of God, has made many of the incredulous laugh, just as the stigmata have caused numerous discussions and publications, but here also science has had to admit its failure. No chemical preparation applied to the wounds for the purpose of disinfecting, and still less tincture of iodine and carbolic acid, can produce the pleasing and particular perfumed odor which emanates from the blood of the wounds as Doctors Festa and Romanelli have confirmed; and further still, they testify that the blood does not become corrupt, as it normally should if it were not an extra-natural phenomena. (30)

The scent often accompanied his person, clothes dipped in his wounds, or even his spiritual presence in a far-off place. According to Fr. Carty, "The perfume is not constant. The opinion of those close to Padre Pio is that whenever anyone notices perfume it is a sign that God bestows some grace through the intercession of Padre Pio."

Every year, thousands of sick people visited Padre Pio, adding to the many sick of San Giovanni Rotundo who lacked proper medical care, and he knew that a miraculous healing was not in God's will for all of them. One day, Padre Pio was saddened to see a sick man lying in the streets for several days because the closest hospital was at least an hour away by automobile. So Padre Pio dreamed of a hospital in San Giovanni Rotondo that would serve them in the spirit of Christian charity, sustained by a community of faithful medical professionals who cared for both the body and the soul. In 1920, he converted an old convent into a tiny hospital to care for the sick, but the unit closed within a few years because it had been stretched thin between high demand and scarce personnel.

For the next decade, Padre Pio struggled to find funds to build a new, state of the art hospital—a feat that would require many millions of dollars and the ability to attract qualified Christian doctors and nurses who would be willing to settle, essentially, in the middle of nowhere. Slowly, benefactors touched by Padre Pio's ministry stepped forward. Padre Pio was able to channel the energies of Emmanuel Brunnato, the man who had investigated Padre Pio's detractors, away from his tendencies to radical politics and questionable business deals to ensure the financial success of the hospital project for the good of the poor.

Padre Pio and his helpers moved forward with plans for the hospital in 1939 but soon had to pause because of World War II. But after the war, a British journalist, Barbara Ward, who was deeply influenced by Padre Pio, secured $400 million from the United Nations Relief and Rehabilitation Administration to complete the project—although the Italian government only delivered a fraction of that money to the hospital.

Nonetheless, Christian doctors and nurses eventually chose to settle in San Giovanni Rotondo and even to forgo earning a salary, granted that their needs and the needs of their families would be addressed by the organization. Starting with the meager but heartfelt donation to the hospital by Mario Gambino, an impoverished father of 10 children, Padre Pio started a fund to ensure that all patients would be able to receive care even if unable to pay or not covered by insurance. Construction began in 1947, and the doors of the hospital, called the House for the Relief of Suffering (*Casa Sollievo della Sofferenza*), finally opened in 1956, admitting patients from all over the region to one of the largest and most state-of-the-art facilities in Italy. Even to the present day, the hospital is able to claim on its website to be "currently one of the most efficient hospitals in Europe." The hospital currently has 1,200 beds, employs 3,000 staff members, and houses an important medical school. It continues to live out Padre Pio's wish: "Now the House for the Relief of Suffering is a small seed, but it will become a mighty oak, a hospital that is a small city and a center for clinical studies of international importance" (Allegri, 199).

In addition to the hospital, Padre Pio inspired a number of other successful initiatives in the world. His prediction of a Capuchin monastery being built in his hometown of Pietrecina was made a reality through the generosity of Maria Pyle, whom he called 'L'Americana.' Maria Pyle came from a wealthy American family and was deeply affected by Padre Pio while spending time in Italy. She chose to dedicate the rest of her life to apostolic work among the poor in San Giovanni Rotundo on behalf of Padre Pio and funded the construction of a Capuchin monastery, church, and school in Pietrecina, which Padre Pio named after the Holy Family. From other funds that came in, Padre Pio established a retirement home for priests and numerous health clinics for the poor.

Also, after Pope Pius XII's call at the dawn of World War II for all people to turn to God in prayer, Padre Pio was inspired to start prayer groups with the help of his spiritual children. Groups of faithful soon emerged throughout the world, inspired to come together in prayer in the spirit and example of Padre Pio, who simply called himself "a monk who prays." Even today, there are 3,000 such prayer groups with three million members.

Later Days

In the late 1940s and early 1950s, money poured in for the construction of the House for the Relief of Suffering, which was becoming a large organization that many wanted to get their hands on. This would lead some to attack Padre Pio's character once again, to discredit him and his leadership of the hospital project. During that time, the friars lost several hundred thousand dollars in a scam hoisted on them and a number of other church organizations by a financier named Gambattista Giuffre, known as "God's banker." He offered extremely high interest rates in return for monetary investments from the Church, only to declare bankruptcy and be off. Though Padre Pio was always suspicious of the man and his selection came about through other friars, the Holy Office was made aware and considered Padre Pio to have mismanaged the funds. Also, accusations that Padre Pio was sexually involved with women were leveled against him once again.

Although Pope Pius XII, who ascended the throne of Peter in 1939, had instructed the Holy Office to cease from harassing Padre Pio, whom he considered to be a holy man, these new accusations brought the friar more trouble from the Vatican. In a series of moves in the early 1950s, the Holy Office placed eight books about Padre Pio on the Index of Forbidden Books, pressured him to transfer the leadership of the hospital, and discouraged devotion to his wounds.

His Capuchin superiors placed a number of further restrictions on his ministry. Aiming to crush the "fanaticism" that Padre Pio's critics accused him of fanning, one of his superiors even forbid him from allowing his Masses to last more than a half hour, from allowing his confessions to last more than three minutes each, from conversing with pilgrims, or even to be given any help by the friars beyond what was given to all. In fact, Padre Pio suffered a serious fall once because the friars were not allowed to assist him up the stairs. The superior went so far as to follow Padre Pio personally in crowds to prevent him from conversing at length with anyone. The crowds were so great that many could not even get into his Masses but could only wait for his blessing from the window in his cell. But Padre Pio had enemies who were waiting to ensnare him; in fact, some of his fellow friars even secretly placed tape recorders inside his confessional, violating the sacred seal of Confession in hopes of making him fall by his own words or actions. They nonetheless found nothing blameworthy. (Allegri, 215–221)

Once again, Emmanuel Brunnato went in to investigate on the behalf of Padre Pio. He found the evidence to clear Padre Pio from the charges and even formed an international organization to come to Padre Pio's defense and distribute the information to clear his name before the international community. Before he was able to testify on Padre Pio's behalf at the United Nations (which had allocated funds for the hospital project) and to disseminate his report broadly, however, the church authorities came to their own conclusion that Padre Pio was innocent and released him of the restrictions on his ministry in the early 1960s. Padre Pio asked Brunnato to stop the efforts to clear his name since it would cause embarrassment to the Church and since he was once again allowed to live the basic life of a friar. This second wave of accusations, however, had clouded a decade of Padre Pio's ministry and curtailed the celebration of the golden jubilee of his priesthood. After all of this, the Holy Office persuaded Padre Pio to sign a document stating that he had never been persecuted by the Vatican or by the Capuchin leadership.

Though Padre Pio had suffered so much all his life, the first sign that his earthly journey might be nearing its end came in 1959 when he was diagnosed with inoperable lung cancer and given only a few months to live. Padre Pio, however, knew that it was not yet his time. As he lay suffering in bed, he wished he could go visit a statue of Our Lady of Fatima that was traveling through Italy for veneration. The priest who accompanied the statue, Fr. Mario Mason, S.J., had tried to arrange for Padre Pio to be present at the ceremony in town, but it was not possible because of the friar's health. So when the statue was being transported away afterward by helicopter, Fr. Mason arranged for the helicopter to stop a few moments over Padre Pio's cell at the monastery at San Giovanni Rotondo. At that moment, Padre Pio cried out to the Blessed Virgin: "Holy Mary, when you came to Italy you confined me to my bed with these illnesses. Now that you are going, are you going to leave me like this?" (Allegri, 240). Just then, his body began to tremble, frightening his caregivers. Our Lady of Fatima, however, had healed Padre Pio in that instant; the tumor was gone, and Padre Pio was soon strong enough to resume his work.

Each day, he pushed himself to keep his schedule of 5 a.m. Mass and long hours of confessions even though his body was slowing down and giving way. Eventually, he even had to be given permission to say Mass sitting down and became confined to a wheelchair. Allegri recounts, "One day when he was forced to stay in bed because it was impossible for him to stand up, he summoned two of his fellow monks and said, 'Come and pull this lazy guy from bed.' He then had them walk him to his confessional" (238). In later days, Padre Pio became rather depressed, introspective, and less jovial; he even wondered whether God was truly pleased with him.

Eternal Glory

It seems that Padre Pio knew for a long while the appointed time for his death. He confided to a friend that it was to be 50 years after he received the permanent stigmata. On the day that he received the stigmata, September 20, 1918, Jesus said to him, "You will bear them for fifty years, and then you will see me" (Allegri, 246). As the time approached, he continued to predict his approaching earthly end. His sufferings became more than he could bear, and he would ask his superior, "Give me the obedience to die." When someone wished him many more years, he replied, "What harm have I ever done to *you*?" (Ruffin, 374). Padre Pio had prayed that the stigmata and the embarrassment it caused would leave him. In the spring of 1968, the stigmata began to fade. As St. Francis lay naked to return simply to the Lord, bearing only that with which he had begun, so Padre Pio would return to the Lord simply and without the renowned, miraculous wounds that he had carried for half a century.

On September 20, 1968, pilgrims gathered at San Giovanni Rotondo to celebrate the fiftieth anniversary of Padre Pio's stigmata. Padre Pio did not join them even though he had carried out his usual priestly duties earlier that day. To his caregivers, his condition seemed not to be a particular cause of concern until it took a turn for the worse overnight. He had a bad asthma attack, but his caregivers were confident he would pull through as usual. Instead, he insisted, "It's over, it's over." Padre Pio made it through the night and was able to celebrate solemn high Mass the next day for the First International Convention of Prayer Groups. He struggled, however, to get through the Mass; he could not continue chanting the prayers of the Mass, having to murmur them instead, and also became confused as to what part of the Mass should come next. After Mass, he stumbled and had to be slowly led away by the friars. As he left, he cried out to the people, "My children, my children!"

That night, he insisted on the continued presence of the friar who was caring for him, and then at 1:30 in the morning, he felt the desire to go out on the veranda to see the stars. He had strength that he had not possessed in a long time as he made his way out with the friar's assistance. He gazed up at the stars, wondering at God's greatness and love, and then hobbled back inside and collapsed on an armchair. He pointed out the portrait of his mother on the wall, telling the friar, "I see two mothers." Together with his earthly mother he saw the Blessed Virgin Mary. As his breathing became labored, he lost color. Despite Padre Pio's protests, the friar went and got help, while Padre Pio continued murmuring "Jesus, Mary." Doctors arrived and gave him injections, realizing that he was having a heart attack. But within a few minutes, his soul had gone on to its reward, to behold the face of God together with St. Francis and all the angels and saints. It was September 23, 1968, or 50 years and three days after Padre Pio had received the sacred stigmata.

At his death, there was no longer any trace of the stigmata whatsoever. Instead, the skin on his hands, feet, and side where the stigmata had been were as fresh as that of a child. In preparing the body, his superiors decided that his hands should be gloved and his feet given slippers so that mourners could see him as they had become accustomed. One hundred thousand people flocked to San Giovanni Rotondo to pay Padre Pio their final respects and to seek his prayers from Heaven.

Blessed Pope Paul VI, who reigned at the time, had great admiration for Padre Pio and had by that time assured the faithful that the friar was innocent of all the slander brought against him. Soon after his election in 1963, he had lifted all the restrictions on Padre Pio and replaced the Capuchin provincial superior (Ruffin, 362). In 1973, Pope Paul VI opened the cause for Padre Pio's beatification at the prompting of the archbishop of Manfredonia and the Polish bishops. The Polish bishops were particularly influenced in their petition by Karol Cardinal Wojtyla, archbishop of Krakow and future Pope St. John Paul II. While still a priest studying in Rome for his doctorate in theology, Wojtyla made a pilgrimage to San Giovanni Rotondo to see Padre Pio and to confess to him. Padre Pio is said to have revealed to him then that one day he would be pope. Years later, Wojtyla would write to Padre Pio for prayers for his good friend, Professor Wanda Poltawska, a mother of four who had terminal throat cancer. Through Padre Pio's prayers, she was miraculously healed (Allegri, 257).

Perhaps embarrassed over their treatment of Padre Pio during his lifetime, the Holy Office stepped in once again to try to halt the beatification process, but Pope Paul VI intervened in Padre Pio's favor. The Sacred Congregation for the Cause of Saints moved forward, collecting all of Padre Pio's letters and writings, and then waited the required 10 years, until 1983, before proceeding to investigate, debate, and discuss the heroic virtues of Padre Pio's life rigorously. For beatification, one confirmed posthumous miracle was needed as a guarantee of Padre Pio's intercession from Heaven—a miracle that would have to be confirmed by multiple disinterested doctors to lack any medical explanation.

Popular during his life, Padre Pio was even more popular among the faithful after death. Already in his lifetime, the church at the Capuchin monastery at San Giovanni Rotondo was not able to accommodate all the pilgrims. The new church of Our Lady of Grace was constructed and finished in 1963, but this also was too small to accommodate the growing number of pilgrims, especially after Padre Pio's death. So the Shrine of Padre Pio, designed to accommodate 10,000 pilgrims for Mass, was finally completed in 2003. Today, the Shrine of Padre Pio is the second-most-visited Catholic shrine in the world. Doubtless, with all of Padre Pio's institutions, San Giovanni Rotondo is no longer the primitive destination that it was when Padre Pio first arrived in 1916.

Padre Pio proved even more powerful in Heaven than on earth, as hundreds of miracles were attributed to him, so finding one was not difficult. In 1999, approximately 200,000 people gathered in St. Peter's Square for Padre Pio's beatification by Pope John Paul II, and after the Vatican's confirmation of a second miracle, 300,000 joined Pope John Paul II for Padre Pio's canonization as a saint. Now officially called St. Pio of Pietrecina, Padre Pio was found in a 2007 survey to be Italy's most popular saint for prayers and intercession. His feast day is September 23rd.

Epilogue

In closing, let us ponder these words St. Padre Pio left us, which show the pattern and spirit of his life:

> Pay little attention to the path on which the Lord places you... But rather, keep your eyes always fixed on he who guides you, and on the heavenly homeland to which he wants to lead you. Why should you worry whether Jesus wants you to reach the homeland by way of the desert or through fields, when one way or the other you will reach blessed eternity just the same?

> Drive away all excessive worry which springs from the trials through which the good Lord wants to visit you, and if this is not possible, drive the thought away and live resigned to divine will in everything. (*Padre Pio's Words of Hope*, edited by Eileen Dunn Bertanzetti, 73)

Padre Pio would not have planned out his life the way that it happened, yet he embraced God's will completely as his life unfolded. Thus, when people came to Padre Pio for prayers and advice, he would often advise them with the approach he himself took: "Pray, hope, and don't worry."

Please enjoy the first two chapters of Pope Francis: Pastor of Mercy, written by Michael J. Ruszala, as available from Wyatt North Publishing.

Pope Francis: Pastor of Mercy

Chapter 1

There is something about Pope Francis that captivates and delights people, even people who hardly know anything about him. He was elected in only two days of the conclave, yet many who tried their hand at speculating on who the next pope might be barely included him on their lists. The evening of Wednesday, March 13, 2013, the traditional white smoke poured out from the chimney of the Sistine Chapel and spread throughout the world by way of television, Internet, radio, and social media, signaling the beginning of a new papacy.

As the light of day waned from the Eternal City, some 150,000 people gathered watching intently for any movement behind the curtained door to the loggia of St. Peter's. A little after 8:00 p.m., the doors swung open and Cardinal Tauran emerged to pronounce the traditional and joyous Latin formula to introduce the new Bishop of Rome: "Annuncio vobis gaudium magnum; habemus papam!" ("I announce to you a great joy: we have a pope!") He then announced the new Holy Father's identity: "Cardinalem Bergoglio..."

The name Bergoglio, stirred up confusion among most of the faithful who flooded the square that were even more clueless than the television announcers were, who scrambled to figure out who exactly the new pope was. Pausing briefly, Cardinal

Tauran continued by announcing the name of the new pope: "...qui sibi nomen imposuit Franciscum" ("who takes for himself the name Francis"). Whoever this man may be, his name choice resonated with all, and the crowd erupted with jubilant cheers. A few moments passed before the television announcers and their support teams informed their global audiences that the man who was about to walk onto the loggia dressed in white was Cardinal Jorge Mario Bergoglio, age 76, of Buenos Aires, Argentina.

To add to the bewilderment and kindling curiosity, when the new pope stepped out to the thunderous applause of the crowd in St. Peter's Square, he did not give the expected papal gesture of outstretched arms. Instead, he gave only a simple and modest wave. Also, before giving his first apostolic blessing, he bowed asking the faithful, from the least to the greatest, to silently pray for him. These acts were only the beginning of many more words and gestures, such as taking a seat on the bus with the cardinals, refusing a popemobile with bulletproof glass, and paying his own hotel bill after his election, that would raise eyebrows among some familiar with papal customs and delight the masses.

Is he making a pointed critique of previous pontificates? Is he simply posturing a persona to the world at large to make a point? The study of the life of Jorge Mario Bergoglio gives a clear answer, and the answer is no. This is simply who he is as a man and as a priest. The example of his thought- provoking gestures flows from his character, his life experiences, his religious vocation, and his spirituality. This book uncovers the life of the 266th Bishop of Rome, Jorge Mario Bergoglio, also known as Father Jorge, a name he preferred even while he was an archbishop and cardinal.

What exactly do people find so attractive about Pope Francis? Aldo Cagnoli, a layman who developed a friendship with the Pope when he was serving as a cardinal, shares the following: "The greatness of the man, in my humble opinion lies not in building walls or seeking refuge behind his wisdom and office, but rather in dealing with everyone judiciously, respectfully, and with humility, being willing to learn at any moment of life; that is what Father Bergoglio means to me" (as quoted in Ch. 12 of Pope Francis: Conversations with Jorge Bergoglio, previously published as El Jesuita [The Jesuit]).

At World Youth Day 2013, in Rio de Janeiro, Brazil, three million young people came out to celebrate their faith with Pope Francis. Doug Barry, from EWTN's Life on the Rock, interviewed youth at the event on what features stood out to them about Pope Francis. The young people seemed most touched by his authenticity. One young woman from St. Louis said, "He really knows his audience. He doesn't just say things to say things... And he is really sincere and genuine in all that he does." A friend agreed: "He was looking out into the crowd and it felt like he was looking at each one of us...." A young man from Canada weighed in: "You can actually relate to [him]... for example, last night he was talking about the World Cup and athletes." A young woman added, "I feel he means what he says... he practices what he preaches... he states that he's there for the poor and he actually means it."

The Holy Spirit guided the College of Cardinals in its election of Pope Francis to meet the needs of the Church following the historic resignation of Pope Benedict XVI due to old age. Representing the growth and demographic shift in the Church throughout the world and especially in the Southern Hemisphere, Pope Francis is the first non-European pope in almost 1,300 years. He is also the first Jesuit pope. Pope Francis comes with a different background and set of experiences. Both as archbishop and as pope, his flock knows him for his humility, ascetic frugality in solidarity with the poor, and closeness. He was born in Buenos Aires to a family of Italian immigrants, earned a diploma in chemistry, and followed a priestly vocation in the Jesuit order after an experience of God's mercy while receiving the sacrament of Reconciliation. Even though he is known for his smile and humor, the world also recognizes Pope Francis as a stern figure that stands against the evils of the world and challenges powerful government officials, when necessary.

The Church he leads is one that has been burdened in the West by the aftermath of sex abuse scandals and increased secularism. It is also a Church that is experiencing shifting in numbers out of the West and is being challenged with religious persecution in the Middle East, Asia, and Africa. The Vatican that Pope Francis has inherited is plagued by cronyism and scandal. This Holy Father knows, however, that his job is not merely about numbers, politics, or even success. He steers clear of pessimism knowing that he is the head of Christ's Body on earth and works with Christ's grace. This is the man God has chosen in these times to lead his flock.

Chapter 2: Early Life in Argentina

Jorge Mario Bergoglio was born on December 17, 1936, in the Flores district of Buenos Aires. The district was a countryside locale outside the main city during the nineteenth century and many rich people in its early days called this place home. By the time Jorge was born, Flores was incorporated into the city of Buenos Aires and became a middle class neighborhood. Flores is also the home of the beautiful Romantic-styled Basilica of San José de Flores, built in 1831, with its dome over the altar, spire over the entrance, and columns at its facade. It was the Bergoglios' parish church and had much significance in Jorge's life.

Jorge's father's family had arrived in Argentina in 1929, immigrating from Piedimonte in northern Italy. They were not the only ones immigrating to the country. In the late nineteenth century, Argentina became industrialized and the government promoted immigration from Europe. During that time, the land prospered and Buenos Aires earned the moniker "Paris of the South." In the late nineteenth and early twentieth centuries waves of immigrants from Italy, Spain, and other European countries came off ships in the port of Buenos Aires. Three of Jorge's great uncles were the first in the family to immigrate to Argentina in 1922 searching for better employment opportunities after World War I. They established a paving company in Buenos Aires and built a four-story building for their company with the city's first elevator. Jorge's father and paternal grandparents followed the brothers in order to keep the family together and to escape Mussolini's fascist regime in Italy. Jorge's father and grandfather also helped with the business for a time. His father, Mario, who had been an accountant for a rail company in Italy, provided similar services for the family business (Cardinal Bergoglio recalls more on the story of his family's immigration and his early life in Ch. 1 of Conversations with Jorge Bergoglio).

Providentially, the Bergoglios were long delayed in liquidating their assets in Italy; this forced them to miss the ship they planned to sail on, the doomed Pricipessa Mafalda, which sank off the northern coast of Brazil before reaching Buenos Aires. The family took the Giulio Cesare instead and arrived safely in Argentina with Jorge's Grandma Rosa. Grandma Rosa wore a fur coat stuffed with the money the family brought with them from Italy. Economic hard times eventually hit Argentina in 1932 and the family's paving business went under, but the Bergoglio brothers began anew.

Jorge's father, Mario, met his mother Regina at Mass in 1934. Regina was born in Argentina, but her parents were also Italian immigrants. Mario and Regina married the following year after meeting. Jorge, the eldest of their five children, was born in 1936. Jorge fondly recalls his mother gathering the children around the radio on Sunday afternoons to listen to opera and explain the story. A true porteño, as the inhabitants of the port city of Buenos Aires are called, Jorge liked to play soccer, listen to Latin music, and dance the tango. Jorge's paternal grandparents lived around the corner from his home. He greatly admired his Grandma Rosa, and keeps her written prayer for her grandchildren with him until this day. Jorge recalls that while his grandparents kept their personal conversations in Piedmontese, Mario chose mostly to speak Spanish, preferring to look forward rather than back. Still, Jorge grew up speaking both Italian and Spanish.

Upon entering secondary school at the age of thirteen, his father insisted that Jorge begin work even though the family, in their modest lifestyle, was not particularly in need of extra income. Mario Bergoglio wanted to teach the boy the value of work and found several jobs for him during his adolescent years. Jorge worked in a hosiery factory for several years as a cleaner and at a desk. When he entered technical school to study food chemistry, Jorge found a job working in a laboratory. He worked under a woman who always challenged him to do his work thoroughly. He remembers her, though, with both fondness and sorrow. Years later, she was kidnapped and murdered along with members of her family because of her political views during the Dirty War, a conflict in the 1970's and 80's between the military dictatorship and guerrilla fighters in which thousands of Argentineans disappeared.

Initially unhappy with his father's decision to make him work, Jorge recalls later in his life that work was a valuable formative experience for him that taught him responsibility, realism, and how the world operated. He learned that a person's self worth often comes from their work, which led him to become committed later in life to promote a just culture of work rather than simply encouraging charity or entitlement. He believes that people need meaningful work in order to thrive. During his boyhood through his priestly ministry, he experienced the gulf in Argentina between the poor and the well off, which left the poor having few opportunities for gainful employment.

At the age of twenty-one, Jorge became dangerously ill. He was diagnosed with severe pneumonia and cysts. Part of his upper right lung was removed, and each day Jorge endured the pain and discomfort of saline fluid pumped through his chest to clear his system. Jorge remembers that the only person that was able to comfort him during this time was a religious sister who had catechized him from childhood, Sister Dolores. She exposed him to the true meaning of suffering with this simple statement: "You are imitating Christ." This stuck with him, and his sufferings during that time served as a crucible for his character, teaching him how to distinguish what is important in life from what is not. He was being prepared for what God was calling him to do in life, his vocation.

Made in the USA
Middletown, DE
02 August 2016